Supervision

Supervision

Bill McKitterick

Open University Press

Open University Press
McGraw-Hill Education
McGraw-Hill House
Shoppenhangers Road
Maidenhead
Berkshire
England
SL6 2QL

email: enquiries@openup.co.uk
world wide web: www.openup.co.uk

and Two Penn Plaza, New York, NY 10121-2289, USA

First published 2012

Copyright © Bill McKitterick, 2012

A catalogue record of this book is available from the British Library

ISBN-13: 978-0-33-524525-3 (pb)
ISBN-10: 0-33-524525-0 (pb)
eISBN: 978-0-33-524526-0

Library of Congress Cataloging-in-Publication Data
CIP data applied for

Typesetting and e-book compilations by
RefineCatch Limited, Bungay, Suffolk
Printed in the UK by CPI Anthony Rowe, Chippenham, Wiltshire

Fictitious names of companies, products, people, characters and/or data that may be used
herein (in case studies or in examples) are not intended to represent any real individual,
company, product or event.

The **McGraw·Hill** Companies

This book is dedicated to all the inspiring social work colleagues I have worked with, from whom I have learned so much and to my mentor and critical friend, Jennifer McKitterick.

Contents

How to use this book

Supervision of social workers is critical to the delivery of safe and effective services, the development of best practice and to support reflective **continuing professional development** (see Glossary). There is a long tradition of professional supervision in social work yet a high proportion of current practitioners report that they do not receive it regularly or that it is not of a good quality. This book provides a pithy, social work resource to enable students and newly qualified social workers, experienced practitioners, supervisors, line managers and leaders to know what good supervision is, how to prepare for and how to use it. It recognizes the current working environment of social workers and their managers, and their shared responsibilities for learning. It includes strategies and advice to protect and prioritize the time and space for supervision.

This book is for all social workers, with a focus on social workers at the start of their professional career, experienced social workers for whom supervision is not working and supervisors and leaders in the profession who are committed to improve supervision. It will also be useful for those managers of social workers who are not social workers themselves, to guide them in how they can ensure the appropriate professional oversight and professional development is provided and assured. Supervision has a special place in the development of social work and yet can be neglected or overshadowed by management and organizational concerns.

This is a book which can be read completely or dipped into. It includes consideration of the complexities of our work and appreciation of the theoretical and historic foundations. The main focus, however, is on practical and workable ways to prepare for and use supervision, ensuring it is given and making improvements if it is not working for you. Good practice points and checklists for easy reference are provided.

Since **reflection** and **critical analysis** (see Glossary) are central to good professional supervision and our own continuing professional development, the book should also be read as a whole, in a quiet time and space. This will help you fully appreciate why supervision is so important, to understand why it is not always as good as it should be and how we can take effective action, in whatever position we are, to put this right.

Chapter 1 sets out the aims of the book and introduces the importance of reflection and continuing professional development as the core of good supervision, both for the social worker and the supervisor.

Chapter 2 examines the functions and activities of supervision, provides a good practice checklist on its importance, why it is essential to maintaining direction and purpose in our work, what I describe as the '**therapeutic imperative**' (see Glossary). There is a checklist for you if your line manager is not a social worker. It also looks at the origins of supervision in order to understand the inherent tensions between professionalism and managerial direction.

Chapter 3 addresses the responsibilities of employers, offers practical advice for employers and managers on supervision policies and procedures, explains how to ensure it takes place and is of good quality, and describes what we should expect in supervision at different stages of our professional career, in different roles and at times of challenge. The professional development of supervisors, managers and leaders is particularly examined. In addition, there is consideration of the emotional components of supervision.

Chapter 4, preparing for supervision, starts with what we can do to help our supervisor, moving on to the full range of 'soft' and 'hard' resources managers and leaders need to put in place. There are tips for both the organization and supervisors, preparation at the different stages of social work careers, including the most experienced practitioners, supervisors, educators, researchers, senior managers and leaders.

Chapter 5 is about what to do when things go wrong, examining the reasons why supervision is not consistently provided, with examples of good and bad practice. There are tips and guidance for both supervisors and social workers with practical advice on problems and solutions and finally where to go if you just cannot find good supervision.

Chapter 6 gives guidance on supervision where the line manager is not a social worker, looking at how this can be accessed and the responsibilities of both the line manager and the employing organization. The chapter also addresses the responsibilities of social workers who formally or informally supervise non-professional staff with whom they are working, looking particularly at delegation and accountability.

A guide to further reading and resources in contained in Chapter 7. There is a glossary on particular specialist terms but jargon has been avoided, and a brief list of references cited in the text is provided.

Supervision is so important that it is worth getting it right. This book explains why it is so important and how to ensure it is provided well, especially at times of great change, enormous service pressure or uncertainty. It should provide the bedrock for our professionalism, our direction and our sense of purpose. It is the sharing of professional development, critical reflection and learning by both the supervisee and the supervisor. When problems arise with supervision, I am confident they can be resolved and I hope this book successfully shows how this can be done.

1 Introduction

Supervision has been at the heart of how we develop and are supported in our practice as social workers. We all remember the supervisors who inspired us and who helped us with almost intolerable work pressures and professional challenges. Social work has a strong tradition of reflective and critical supervision, distinct from managerial oversight or performance management. Social work has a growing body of knowledge and skills which are not always well articulated or addressed. Supervision provides the structure and the discipline for both the supervisor and the supervisee to collaborate in progressive learning and to demonstrate accountability as skilful and effective professionals.

The aims of this book are to do the following:

■ support good practice in supervision;
■ assist in preparing for supervision;
■ help improve supervision when it is not going well;
■ get supervision started again when it has fallen into disuse or been over-shadowed by management tasks or work pressures;
■ manage the reflective and development of the practice skills components of supervision alongside the organizational focus on performance management;
■ consider its place within multi-professional settings and our responsibilities working with non-professional colleagues.

The book is for all social workers, including supervisors, managers, educators, researchers and leaders. In addition, line managers of social workers who are not social workers themselves will find it useful in identifying what social workers need for their professional development and what will secure good practice.

Reflective supervision is not a one-way process, at best, it is mutual learning, with a fellow professional as a peer. My first experience was as a student with a practice teacher who was in training analysis, who brought reflective calm and encouraged me to learn, whose guidance was gentle, clear and challenging. Her expectations of what I should learn were limitless. My current peer supervision is equally challenging, focused on critical analysis, on reflecting on what I do, what I can change and what I cannot. The sharing of new learning and new thinking is at its core.

High quality reflective supervision, including regular review of the development of our professional practice skills, is the most important way of ensuring that we deliver high quality and effective social work to the people we serve. It ensures that we carry out our duties according to best practice standards, current research in effective practice, policies and procedures.

As social workers at the start of our professional career we have much to learn and will need the time, energy, resources and commitment of employers and line managers for support, to enable autonomy to be earned in becoming seasoned professionals (Donnellan and Jack 2010). In return, at that stage of our career we bring enthusiasm, current practice research knowledge and an uninhibited passion for the profession we have just joined. It is shameful when this energy and the investment in gaining the professional status are only rewarded by poor quality or infrequent supervision. This is demonstrated in studies and surveys, for example, 17 per cent of new social work graduates report receiving supervision less than once a month (Sharpe et al. 2011).

Service inspectorates identify supervision as key to the delivery of good services. Ofsted (2012: 17) cites supervision and line management support as the most important form of support for assuring good outcomes for children and young people:

Senior managers played an important role in facilitating a strong supervision culture through:

- clear standards and policies
- ensuring supervision was well resourced
- modelling the behaviours required of effective supervision, including acknowledging their own struggles
- scrutinizing and challenging plans and decisions
- providing well-timed training for first line managers
- access to independent staff counselling services
- systematic audit of supervision practice.

All employers providing a social work service must have a supervision policy for social workers that makes sure the particular responsibilities social workers have are met and that their specific professional development needs are assured. Equally, employers must ensure all supervisors are well trained, prepared for their responsibilities and that their skills and knowledge are kept refreshed.

Employers need to develop a systematic method of ensuring supervision, of high quality, is provided regularly. This needs to be coupled with planning the **continuing professional development** (see Glossary) of the whole of their social work workforce, from the most senior leaders to the newest recruit to the profession.

Social workers and their supervisors are registered professionals, responsible for their own practice and development. We are responsible for preparing and planning for supervision and ensuring our own development needs are met. Senior and experienced social workers also need to ensure they continually enhance their knowledge and skills, critically reflecting on how they are working as a member of the profession. This includes those in the most senior management and leadership positions, directors, heads of service, independent reviewing officers, chairs of panels and case conferences responsible for protecting children and vulnerable adults. Practice teachers, university teachers and researchers equally have to develop their practice skills and knowledge. The form of their supervision may be different but the content and the agenda remain the same. Independent social workers and those who work through agencies need to pay particularly close attention to how they receive supervision. It is imperative that they assure the quality of their practice and continuing professional development and are ready to demonstrate this to those who commission their services.

This book is written at a time when our profession is growing in confidence and ambition for excellence, with the potential for the development of a single independent College of Social Work in the United Kingdom. The profession can wrest the leadership of social work from the numerous organizations who prescribe formulaic ways of working and the unhelpful managerialist culture. The audit language of efficiency, effectiveness and economy, embedded in service performance assessments by the Local Government Act 1999, confirmed a growing focus on prescribed performance indicators and formulaic working methods which have reduced individual judgement and independent critical thinking among many public sector professionals. The term for this is '**managerialism**' (see Glossary). This idea is based on an assumption that general management methods are of prime importance for a good service and the particular knowledge, skills and experience needed to deliver the service are of secondary importance. Systems, prescribed ways of working and loss of discretion and creativity risk becoming embedded in the working environment of social work. This has been challenged by the **Munro Review** (2011) (see Glossary) and exposed as a risk to good and effective services. Good and effective management is a vital component of social work services, but when management by performance indicators dominates, the professional skills and potential of social work are squeezed or kept out. The paradox is that social workers can become deskilled, or never develop effective practice skills which achieve change, and consequently can be seen to need more direction on process and more oversight and scrutiny.

Supervision is the place where knowledge, skills, evaluation of evidence, critical analysis and **reflection** (see Glossary) are shared, maintained and enhanced. Performance management can be used as a tool for effective practice, it is not an end in itself.

The current architecture of organizations, coupled with government guidance have to articulate practice standards or foster ownership within the profession of their diverse prescribed policies. They have failed to give authority to, or allow significant influence from the direct experience of those in practice and those leading social work services. The Social Work Taskforce Final Report (2009: para. 1.32) identified that social work qualifying training 'is currently founded on standards and requirements set by different bodies, which are confusing and lack transparency. As such they provide weak levers for a concerted effort to drive up the quality.'

The reason why the Social Work Taskforce Final Report (2009) and the Munro Review of Child Protection (2011) have been so welcome is that they articulate, and indeed trumpet, many messages well known within our profession and services, but the responsible organizations have been impervious to these calls and have not listened. Social work has not had the confidence to articulate coherent and credible service standards. We collectively need to focus on identifying and upholding best practice, based on good evidence and take responsibility for our professional development at all levels.

There can be a tendency for us all to agree to think supervision is a 'good thing' without ensuring it really takes place as an integral part of our professionalism, not simply a method of management. It is vital if we wish to provide an effective social work service. It is specific to social work and social work responsibilities and skills. It is a meeting of professional peers, and is where the particular skills, evidence and judgements of social work practice are rehearsed, analysed and articulated.

2 What is supervision?

Professional supervision is a central part of how we work as social workers and how our employers and managers support us in providing a good social work service. It can be easy to avoid when pressures of work are high or we are facing changes in how our services are organized. At these times supervision is even more important for us all. We and our supervisors need to work particularly hard to stop the opportunities for supervision slipping as we are too busy or preoccupied.

Let's start with what supervision should be.

Good Practice Point: Essential Functions in Supervision

1 Shared critical analysis and reflection, including consideration of relevant research.
2 Shared decision-making on individual cases, where policies determine the social worker is not singly responsible.
3 Identifying any changes required in your work to enable you to provide a good service.
4 Development of your professional knowledge and skills.
5 Planning and reviewing your continuing professional development.
6 Assuring the quality and effectiveness of your practice and the service you provide.

This list shows the range of work which needs to be covered. You and your supervisor need to keep the supervision agenda balanced. It may be that all aspects cannot be covered in every session but if you find that some areas are regularly missed, it is important to address this with your supervisor.

It is useful to consider the differences and similarities between supervision and an ordinary meeting with a line manager. The first functions and activities in the good practice point list above relate to you as a professional, working with your supervisor as a peer, albeit one who is more senior and probably more experienced. If as a newly qualified social worker, you have previously worked in social care, you will have moved into a professional role, with greater personal responsibility and with specific skills to provide a different service and range of interventions. Supervision includes shared learning and shared responsibilities. It is a meeting of two professionals, albeit one in a supervisory role, but with a growing level of autonomy earned by the social worker and therefore growing authority within the relationship.

Example from Practice

Becky, a newly qualified social worker, was appointed to a new post responsible for drug misuse. It was a new area of work for me as her supervisor and there was a real challenge in seeking to broaden the related medical services beyond a nearly exclusively one of methadone prescription. We learned and explored the service issues and the challenges together. I learned far more from he in her enthusiastic quest for knowledge, and developing social work skills in this specialist service. it was peer learning at its best.

One way of understanding the different aspects of supervision is to look at its functions as *normative, formative* and *restorative*. According to Donnellan and Jack (2010: 140), these three aspects of supervision reflect different areas to focus upon:

1   *normative*: organizational or managerial (focus on the organization);

2 *formative*: educational or developmental (focus on the social worker);

3 *restorative*: personal or supportive (focus on the social worker).

It also is useful to look at how supervision has been described for all staff in children's and social care services. Morrison (2005) states that the four objectives of supervision for social care staff are:

1 competent, accountable performance/practice (management function);

2 continuing professional development (development function);

3 personal support (support function);

4 engaging the individual with the organization (mediation function).

The additional activities we need in our supervision as professional social workers are *reflection, shared critical analysis* and consideration of *practice research evidence*. The breadth and depth of our responsibilities we have as social workers are highlighted where our supervisor, who is a manager and a professional social worker, has responsibilities to make particular case decisions. Examples of these are:

■ taking the decision on whether the threshold for instituting formal safeguarding procedures has been reached for a child or vulnerable adult;

■ assuring an effective plan of intervention is in place to protect vulnerable people;

■ allocating scarce resources based on the assessments and judgements made by social workers.

These examples highlight the dynamic of the supervision process where the supervisor is entering into reflection and critical thinking, in order to make a professional decision. This is a mutual, shared process, unlike a traditional line managerial relationship. It is the collaboration of two professionals. In the supervision session, both you and your supervisor are actively sharing your critical analysis. You as the social worker are helping them to come to their own professional judgements. Your supervisor needs to recognize and use your professional authority and expertise in reaching their own decisions. They will have used the shared reflection and joint critical analysis to come to their decisions, for which they are responsible both as a social worker and as a manager.

SUPERVISION AS PERSONAL SUPPORT

A definition of 35 years ago has a somewhat literary, florid and emotionally focused description of what supervision should be. According to Kadushin (1976: 229), supervision should do the following:

- allay anxiety;
- reduce guilt;
- increase certainty;
- relieve dissatisfaction;
- fortify flagging faith;
- affirm and reinforce the worker's assets;
- replenish depleted self-esteem;
- nourish and enhance the capacity for adaptation;
- alleviate psychological pain;
- restore emotional equilibrium;
- comfort;
- bolster and refresh.

This description has stood the test of time and is a reasonable expectation for you to have as a social worker, and a good reminder to your supervisor of what they should be giving. It is the standard we should all aspire to for all supervision. Later we will look in detail at how we can ensure we receive this, even if at times it seems unachievable.

To need and expect support is not a sign of weakness or lack of competence, it is the mark of a true professional who demands the resources to do a good job.

LOOKING AT OTHER PROFESSIONS

In health service professions there has been a growing culture of what is termed 'clinical supervision'. This recognizes the location of many staff in multi-professional teams and the necessity of assuring standards of practice and judgements where professional autonomy is expected. Everyone expects supervision to be provided by one of their own profession: 'Clinical supervision is a designated interaction between two or more practitioners within a safe and supportive environment that enables a continuum of reflective critical analysis of care, to ensure quality patients' services and the well being of the practitioner' (Bishop 2007).

Psychiatrists have a clear expectation for supervision in their early professional development, one hour of protected time each week, from an accredited supervisor (Cope 2010). The profession is clear that good supervision must include clinical management, teaching, research and pastoral care.

Counselling and psychotherapists, as one would expect, have requirements and expectations of supervision. It should involve: 'reflexive explorations and development of helping practice, in a supportive yet challenging context' (Bond et al. 2010).

Good Practice Point: Why Supervision is Important

Supervision does the following:

■ Supports social workers in contributing to the delivery of an effective, good quality social work service.

- Promotes the practice of the social worker as an agent of change and maximizes the capacity of the people who use their service to lead independent and fulfilling lives.
- Ensures competent and accountable performance.
- Provides the focus for reflection and critical analysis on practice in individual casework, exploring new ways of working and in the development of specific practice skills.
- Addresses the inherent emotional challenge of social work; many of the people we serve tend to be the most excluded and have often been rejected by other services as being too challenging, too difficult and too hard to help.
- Promotes and supports continuing professional development, ensuring that planned individual development needs are met, including current research knowledge, new practice skills and accessing **post-qualifying awards** (see Glossary).
- Shares case and key decision-making accountability, where the social worker may not carry this alone, due to their experience or where practice guidance determines case decisions are held elsewhere.
- Assures effective recruitment and retention of social workers.
- Engages the social worker in the organization where they work.

IF YOUR SUPERVISOR IS NOT A SOCIAL WORKER

However, you may work in a setting where your supervisor or line manager is not a registered social worker. Both the social worker and their employer must ensure that there is direct and regular access to professional supervision by a registered social worker and that there are clear policies for the allocation of responsibilities for supervision and line management. In many joint health and social care settings there will be specific arrangements made for 'clinical supervision' for the health professionals which will need to be adapted for social workers. They will form the basis of the organization's standards for social workers. It will also be important to consider the relative seniority of the 'head of profession' for social work alongside that for other professions. In addition, some health professions have a more established, embedded, structured culture and infrastructure for continuing professional development, which all social workers, including their managers need to emulate and ensure equivalent resources are made available.

You may work in a setting where you are the only social worker, or be only one of a very few members of any profession which value their specific developmental needs. In these circumstances it is especially important to get the right kind of supervision, especially early in your career and professional development in order to ensure you have the very best start.

Good Practice Checklist: if Your Supervisor is not a Social Worker

✓ Ask what the arrangements are for providing 'off-line' supervision from a registered social worker.

✓ Find out what arrangements colleagues from other professions have for their supervision and professional development.

✓ If there is not standard system in place, check with your line manager if a special arrangement can be made for you to have a social work supervisor.

✓ Actively build your social work professional network for peer support, discussion of professional issues and access to professional development opportunities.

✓ Remember it is part of your professionalism to have supervision from a social worker, it is not a sign of neediness or dependence.

WE ALL NEED PROFESSIONAL SUPERVISION

In independent practice, however experienced and self-confident as a social worker you are, regular and challenging supervision remains an imperative. It is needed to foster critical analysis, to ensure high standards of practice and to assure continuing professional development. Without this, we cannot demonstrate our competence and assure others we are entitled to a relatively high degree of professional autonomy.

A range of management, leadership, university teaching and research posts are held by social workers who should retain their professional registration and who need to ensure that their own professional skills and knowledge are maintained to a high standard. In these positions we have a challenge in retaining our expertise in the service for which we are responsible. While we may not have a traditional caseload, we often have case responsibilities which make it necessary for us to identify how we systematically ensure the discharge of our responsibilities as social workers and leaders in our profession and how our work is overseen and critically reviewed. This is distinct from performance as managers, educators or researchers. We need a range of challenging mentoring, peer review and structured professional development to be in place.

SUPERVISION EARLY IN OUR CAREER

Across the UK, national schemes for newly qualified social workers, with clear expectations of good supervision, protected time for professional development and appropriate allocation of work, have developed rather slowly. While these standards have not always been met, they will become more and more part of our normal way of working. In addition, some regulatory inspections have given this area particular attention. My own experience is that it is easy to see a service heading for failure when it does not properly supervise and support social workers early in their career. I have found it a good barometer of overall service quality.

The supervision of social workers early in their career requires particular attention. It can be a most isolated and challenging time, away from the peer support of fellow students, the learning resources of the university and the protected time and space for discussion and discovery. You may find your new colleagues are jaded and cynical, and it takes time to find people who share your enthusiasms and interests. Whatever you do, do not despair, most of your new colleagues will welcome the breath of fresh air you bring. Your different and new perspectives and your awareness of new research and ideas from your time at university will be a tonic. Those sad souls who try to pull you down into their 'real world' are the people who need you most! They need your inspiration and optimism.

If you are returning to a team or service where you have worked before in an unqualified post, you will need to hold on hard to your new professional status. A 'prophet in their own country' is always a difficult position to be in, but do persevere and practise and explore the new, different skills and knowledge you have acquired. You have not studied at university to gain a ticket for more recognition while you do the same work; you are different now. Your qualification is not a ticket to travel to one place, it is a passport to a lifetime of professional development and growth.

The foundations for good practice include preparing well for supervision and learning to use it effectively. We need to establish these good habits at the outset of our working career as a social worker. Currently a proportion of social work students will not have received supervision from a social worker in all their practice placements, due to recent reductions in standards. Consequently, for them, the experience of social work supervision will be a new one. Fortunately this is being rectified by the **Social Work Reform Board** (see Glossary) and will no longer be the case after 2013 for the final practice placement and

2014 for all placements. Some newly qualified social workers may have had limited experience as students of working in a setting where other social workers are employed. Others may have had little practice experience or education in the specialist work area where they are employed.

None of this is a bar to building a successful career. With careful thought in the first sessions of supervision, in your development plan and in your induction, these gaps in experience and knowledge can be remedied.

Studies of the provision of supervision show an enduring and worrying pattern of non-delivery. In the children's services newly qualified social worker pilot programme in England, Carpenter et al. (2010: 25) reported that:

> On average they received supervision for 90 minutes every two weeks; this was the requirement for the first three months of the programme, after which it may be reduced to monthly supervision. Four in ten reported receiving supervision of less than 90 minutes and/or their supervisions were less frequent. The remaining ten per cent said they had not been receiving it at all.

This is all the more alarming when the substantial special government funding provided to employers for this pilot is taken into account.

The Social Work Reform Board commissioned a workload survey of social workers in all sectors and found that 'Just under two thirds (63 percent) said they received supervision at least every four weeks, with just over one in ten saying it happened more frequently' (Baginsky et al. 2009).

Service inspection reports have also regularly cited the lack of regular supervision of social workers as a key problem. The key failings found by inspectors in children's services were summarized in 2001. Gordon and Hendry (2001: 153), found the problems included:

- infrequent and unstructured supervision with interruptions;
- inadequate recording of supervision;
- lack of expertise and specialist knowledge of supervisors;
- lack of rigour in ensuring compliance with policies and procedures;
- failure to challenge decisions and lack of rigour in examining the basis for decisions;
- failure to record decisions on cases or to routinely monitor case files;
- failure to address the professional development needs of workers.

The evidence of failure to embed consistent good standards and practice should not depress you. It shows that if you are not receiving good, regular and helpful supervision, you are not alone. It must inspire us all to take control, to promote and uphold the standards which are core to our profession and our professionalism.

Do not allow your own poor supervision to be excused by this evidence, use it to challenge and to show how harmful it is. In Chapter 5, 'When things go wrong', the reasons behind these consistent findings are examined and practical steps are described to address the problems.

THE THERAPEUTIC IMPERATIVE FOR SOCIAL WORK PRACTICE

Social work practice is dynamic, it is relationship-based, with achieving change and empowerment at its heart. While there is a tendency in some settings to focus on using social workers to undertake assessments, or arrange services provided by others and to review the function of **case management** (see Glossary), these are not exclusively social work tasks and should never be to the exclusion of the essentially therapeutic, relationship-based responsibilities of the profession. There is an imperative to make a difference. The competent and skilled social worker provides direct help through their own intervention, using a range of specific social work methods and knowledge, Farmer (2009), in her study of patterns of social work interventions and outcomes when reuniting looked-after children with their parents, identifies 'proactive and purposeful' practice as a key factor for good outcomes. It is worth holding on to those inspiring words: 'proactive and purposeful'. In the formulaic procedures under legislation for services for children, this same work may be described as assessing the suitability of the parents, assessing risks and reviewing how the child is progressing back with their own family. However, these are only a part of the social work to be undertaken. They provide only a frame-work. The real work is in identifying what both the parents and the children want and need, within a positive relationship, providing the appropriate emotional support, advice and assistance and, where necessary, fighting like a tiger to get the family the help needed from others.

Another area of social work practice which can be dominated by frameworks and protocols is working with an elderly person in hospital, and their family, who is not considered able to return to their own home. The framework for the work entails gathering information from health service professionals and family members, and assessing eligi-bility for public funding for residential and nursing home care. For the person at the centre of all this, the elderly person surrounded by busy hospital staff who identify them as a 'bed-blocker' and by relatives who fear for their loved one's future, and who face the personal terror of not coping in their own home, this is one of the biggest decisions of their lives and probably the last big decision they will ever make. The social worker's role is more than judging service eligibility. The feelings of loss and powerlessness are real. The strains and guilt within families need expression and consideration. The hospital will need firm encour-agement not to give up on treatments and care which can increase independence. The elderly person at the centre is likely to need time and space to consider how they wish to use their own personal budget for personal care. The social worker can help them come to their own decision, rather than give in to those around them.

Example from Practice

A few years ago, when the health service was drastically reducing its 'continuing care' beds for elderly people and identifying patients as 'bed blockers', a wise hospital social worker described to me his main responsibility was making time for people to make the right decisions. My own experience over many years of talking with people who have recently been admitted to long-term residential and nursing home care is that the large majority regret the move and they have told me they made the decision under pressure. It is a hard area of work but the social worker has a critical role in helping those who can regain some independence, for however short a period of time, with perhaps a degree of heightened risk, and help people come to their own decisions. Case management may demand assessment against eligibility criteria and performance targets may demand clearing hospitals of bed blockers, but there is more to social work than this.

As social workers faced with formal assessment procedures and processes, we can come to see ourselves as primarily assessors. This is a form of collusion with the authors of procedures who believe that if all we do is prescribed in print, good services will be delivered. We all can forget the centrality of our relationship with the people we are working with. In our work we have conversations about clarifying feelings, exploring options to solve problems, the expression of despair, loss and hope; we share advice and information, we help people navigate the complex and confusing world of public and private services. This is a personal relationship.

The Munro Review (Munro 2011) has been a timely challenge:

> The professional account of social work practice 'in which relationships play a central role' appears to have been gradually stifled and replaced by a managerialist account that is fundamentally different.

The managerialist approach has been called a 'rational-technical approach', where the emphasis has been on the conscious, cognitive elements of the task of working with children and families, on collecting information, and making plans.

This heralds a new time of shared learning and the release of old passions and new skills, for us as social workers and supervisors. The explicit shared, mutual learning is an aspect of good supervision which fosters respect and ensures the supervisor never forgets that they too are still developing in their professional practice skills and knowledge. We will inevitably spend part of our time simply gathering information or refusing a service to some people. We need to remember at all times we seek to make a difference, this is what I call the **therapeutic imperative** (see Glossary). If we are not making a difference, then our skills as a social worker are not needed.

The Origins of Supervision in Social Work

There are two strands in the history of social work. One is the administration of welfare and charitable assistance, and the other is psychodynamic therapy and counselling. Both of them bring an expectation of structured supervision but each tradition brings its own distinct or different content and function.

The first tradition is the administration of welfare through charity organizations in the United Kingdom and the United States of America. This developed into outdoor relief and later into state benefits from public sector organizations (Burnham 2011). The continuity and persistence of this tradition are seen in the oversight of case management, assessment of eligibility for services and performance measurement through targets.

The second tradition shines through in critical analysis, shared reflection and the centrality of relationship-based practice. This is also combined with our profession's ambition and hunger for continuing and progressive professional development.

Both traditions are strong on ensuring the quality and accountability of practice and both need to be covered in supervision. The challenge for us is how to recognize, acknowledge and address both. Within our work, as practitioners, supervisors and leaders, we need to remember the two very different cultures and sources of potency which can conflict, often in the exercise of power and authority. This is part of our territory, where we live and operate, as social workers and where the people we serve live and how they receive our service.

SUPERVISION AS A PLACE FOR LEARNING

The shared and mutual learning in supervision has already been identified above. The two social workers in supervision, the supervisor and supervisee, are both learners. We are peers, colleagues and collaborators. A supervisor has to have a good understanding of the differences between 'learning behaviour' and 'practice learning'. Learning behaviour is focused on how we as a social worker are learning – how our learning skills are enhanced and developed. Inevitably our supervisor has a role as an educator but we will be learning too through experience, reading, from discussion with our peers and in formal training. Evidence of 'practice learning' will be seen in our growing ability to practise effectively as a social worker. In order for us to prepare for a career-long journey of informed and improving practice, we have to develop our capacity in both learning and practice skills.

Good Practice Point: Elements of Learning

There are four elements of learning required within the supervision process, which apply equally to the supervisee and the supervisor:

1 Reflection, the thoughtful and shared critical analysis of information which is available, the review of intuitive judgements and of relevant research evidence.
2 Gaining knowledge, including the ability to evaluate research on what works and reviewing formal training received.
3 Development of practice skills to intervene as a social worker to achieve change.
4 Development of the ability to process complex information and knowledge, to cogently analyse and to express in written and verbal communication.

It is useful to consider ourselves and to discuss with our supervisor on a regular basis how we are keeping the balance between all four of these aspects of our learning. This learning is consistent with the skills and abilities which are identified as **'graduateness'** in higher education (see Glossary). These are identified as managing tasks and solving problems, working with others, communication and self-awareness. The current emphasis on reflection in much social work education literature is welcome but can overshadow practice knowledge and skills in social work intervention. In principle, reflective learning should be the glue for the other three, helping us to grow as social workers who are continuing learners in knowledge and practice skills.

We work in busy environments and the work pressures and demands can seem voracious and insatiable. Part of us loves the adrenalin rush of the busy team and the crisis. All this emphasis on reflection, learning and thoughtful protected supervision can feel like a luxury and separate from the real world. Even some of the language can seem academic and remote.

How does the reflective social worker move to conclusions and to action? How do we guard against analysis paralysis? Points 2 and 4 above are the traditional expectations of graduateness; point 3 is the stuff of social work practice.

There is a long-standing lack of agreement within our profession on the responsibility of social workers to achieve change by their own direct intervention through a range of advocacy, therapy or community action. I would argue that this feeds our reticence about identifiable practice skills. The emphasis on social work 'values' as the special thing that only social work brings to the multi-disciplinary party, presumptuously implies others do not own or act upon the same values. Perniciously these values often crowd out the identification and application of the skills which social workers need to successfully help the people they serve to achieve change. It is pretentious and arrogant for us to claim our values are distinct or reserved to social work; most other professions have similar values statements and ethical standards. They do not stop them doing other things as well!

THE ADMINISTRATIVE AND THE RELATIONSHIP TRADITIONS OF SOCIAL WORK

In supervision and management, social workers meet these traditions together, side by side, sometimes distinct, sometimes confusingly coalesced and sometimes one dominated or swallowed up by the other. Tsui (2005) examines the administrative tradition of social work, which has been particularly strong in statutory settings and is closely linked to determining eligibility to social care and other specialist services. Clearly, resources for services are finite and decision-making on eligibility and rationing needs to be objective and with accountability clear. The management of risk, safeguarding and protection are key responsibilities of social workers. Again, the making of judgements and decisions needs careful consideration, with accountability clear. Where social work services focus their energies and resources on mass screening and assessing for service eligibility and for risk, the opportunities and the emphasis on relationship-based social work is in danger of being minimized. It is also interesting to reflect on what word we should use to describe the people we serve. Can a person be a 'service user' or 'client' if we merely assess their needs and then do not provide a service?

One of the ways of looking at this is to consider two opposing forces in the world in which we operate as social workers: (1) the cluster of forces of administration, managerialism and performance; and (2) the cluster of professionalism, thoughtful practice and relationship-based practice (Figure 2.1). These need to be both reconciled in supervision as important, but essentially distinct sets of activities, allowing neither to dominate or crowd out the other. The real skill of the professional social worker, in both giving and receiving supervision, is to bring the two forces together, using those on the left to help deliver those on the right, never ever letting those on the left dominate.

The essence of good supervision is to use the numerous external and internal systems and procedures to assure good and safe practice, without them pushing professional judgement, the earning of greater autonomy, reflection, **critical analysis** (see Glossary) and the development of growing skills and knowledge off the supervision agenda. The therapeutic and developmental origins of social work support the whole agenda. Our own ownership and responsibility for the whole agenda become progressively more important as we become more experienced, whether in our roles in practice, leadership or in education.

In this chapter we have examined what supervision is and why it is important for all of us throughout our careers, however experienced we are and whatever our responsibilities. Social work is not an administrative role, however mired we may feel at times by procedures and legal process. Our responsibility is to achieve change, whether by promoting independence, helping people to be safe and to achieve their ambitions, to help heal pain or changing how organizations and those in power treat people. While there are administrative and management functions which supervision can address and are a part of its origins, the danger is that these can dominate and exclude the fundamental imperative of professional development and learning.

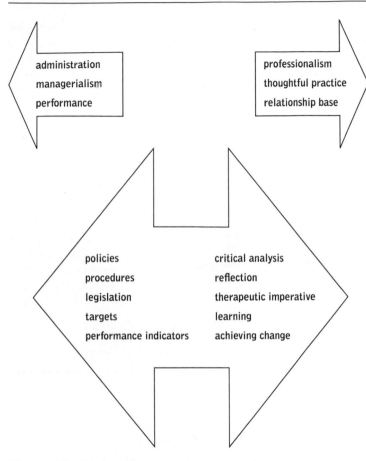

administration
managerialism
performance

professionalism
thoughtful practice
relationship base

policies
procedures
legislation
targets
performance indicators

critical analysis
reflection
therapeutic imperative
learning
achieving change

Figure 2.1 The opposing forces in social work

3 Responsibilities and standards in supervision

It is important to start with what we should reasonably expect from supervision. This is both to ensure we play our part in participating and are clear what we are looking for in choosing our employer. We should have ambitious expectations, based on the standards of our profession and be ready to play our full part in securing it if it is not available or is of poor quality. Supervisors, senior managers and leaders have clear accountabilities and are responsible through their own professional status as social workers for ensuring that good arrangements are in place. They are responsible for quality assurance to secure it and they are responsible for it underpinning high quality social work practice.

An employer who wishes to both attract and retain good social workers has to ensure they provide the working environment which enables and supports safe practice.

Good Practice Box: a Good Employer

The following should be provided by a good employer:

■ a supervision standard for social workers, at all stages of their career and professional development;
■ clear and professional development and career pathways, linked to induction and post-qualifying awards;
■ supervision agreements and personal development plans, formally and regularly reviewed;
■ a culture that combats busy-itis and provides a 'sacred space' for supervision and professional development;

- high quality training which has elements which are multi-disciplinary and elements which are specific to social work;
- training and refresher courses for supervisors;
- quality assurance and audit of supervision.

What makes supervision particularly important for social work is the complexity of the information we work with and the uncertainties of what will make a difference. This is the therapeutic imperative, how we make a difference, the need to move forward from assessment and care management to a greater focus on social work methods and intervention in a regime of continuing professional development. Social workers must analyse and then manage the different and often conflicting needs of adults with complex and extensive care requirements, those of their different family members and sometimes the wider community. This requires analytical and reflective skills of a high order. This is clearly a challenge especially when you consider that we can never fully predict or be certain of what will prevent future harm or improve life chances. There is an unwelcome paradox here. The adoption of universal staff supervision policies in social care and children's services has distracted us from rigorous basic supervision standards for social workers. The focus should be on the extent and complexity of their specific skills and responsibilities.

Good Practice Checklist: Choosing your Employer

✓ Do they have a policy on induction for supervision of social workers?

✓ Does the policy include arrangements for validated continuing professional development, perhaps with specific reference to access to post-qualifying awards?

✓ Is your supervisor a registered social worker and, if not, are there arrangements for you to have regular planned professional supervision from one?

✓ What special arrangements have been made for the Assessed and Supported Year in Employment (ASYE)?

KEY ELEMENTS OF A GOOD SUPERVISION POLICY

Most employers have a supervision policy for social workers, though you may find it is out of date or your social worker colleagues and your supervisor are unaware of it. Feel confident to ask and to challenge.

It is not hard to update a supervision policy, or to prepare one for the first time. Seeking copies of the policies of other social work employers is helpful and they can easily be adapted to local needs. It is important to use the expertise and experience of social workers at all levels of experience and seniority from within the employing organization. Their ownership of the policy and direct engagement in any revisions and audit will encourage compliance and their contribution to quality assurance. The contribution of first line managers is particularly important as they carry the main responsibility. The policy must meet their needs and match their capacity, in terms of both time and skills. The expectations the policy has of them have to be resourced and prioritized among all their other roles and responsibilities. The policy needs to be owned by the director and its implementation and oversight led by the senior manager for social work services.

The policy must be tailored to social workers, and where there is a generic supervision policy for different groups or all staff, a particular section is needed with specifications within it for social workers. This is required to ensure our exacting professional development needs are met and that we receive the support and oversight for our particular accountabilities. The responsibilities of supervisors and social workers to plan and prepare for supervision should be set out clearly.

Resourcing training in supervision and leadership of practice for prospective supervisors and managers, induction once in post and refresher courses are a vital part of the agency policy.

Good Practice Checklist: Key Components of the Supervision Policy

✓ Clear statement on function.
✓ Arrangements for leadership, audit and quality assurance.
✓ Responsibilities of both supervisors and supervisees.
✓ Frequency and length, proportionate to experience and seniority.
✓ Model supervision agreement and arrangements for at least an annual review.
✓ Model personal development plan.
✓ Recording supervision.
✓ Supervisor training and refresher courses.
✓ Arrangements for specific validated and progressive training for social workers.

Let us now look in detail at the supervision agreement.

THE SUPERVISION AGREEMENT AND RECORDING SUPERVISION

Making a written record of supervision is the responsibility of the supervisor, who should provide a copy for the social worker. It may be helpful for both of you to sign and date these. There needs to be clarity on who can have access to the record. Case decisions will need to be recorded in case files. The supervision policy needs to be clear how the records should be used for supervision, quality assurance or audit purposes. Where formal performance or disciplinary processes have been started, it is advisable to record these in separate documents, recognizing they have a specific purpose and may need to be stored separately. Nevertheless these records should be shared with the supervisee and they should have a copy. This is to retain the openness and trust which are essential to supervision. The records of the reviews of supervision and the personal development plans should include planned and achieved professional development. This is both important for planning workforce development and for the record of continuing professional development for renewal of professional registration. A standard format for the supervision agreement record of supervision and review is valuable but the supervisor should be given discretion in how to use this. Too much standardization can unintentionally make good recording less likely and will stifle creativity and professional discretion.

Good Practice Box: Elements of the Supervision Agreement

- A short résumé of the functions of supervision and the expectations of preparation by the supervisor and supervisee.
- The balanced agenda of addressing casework, shared reflection and continuing professional development.
- Resources available for social work professional development, including access to validated learning.
- Frequency and length of supervision sessions.
- Arrangements to replace missed sessions.
- How supervision is recorded.
- Dates for formal review of supervision and personal professional development.

It may be useful to have a model agenda for supervision as an *aide-mémoire* to ensure all aspects are covered and reviewed, for example:

- starting with sharing what each wants from the session;
- confirming what must be achieved by the end;
- case and service discussion, shared critical analysis and reflection, consideration of relevant research, making key decisions;
- review of key service performance issues and identifying how the supervisor will help;
- identification and review of professional development needs and how they are being delivered;
- planning for the next session and fixing the date and time for it.

This is addressed in more detail in Chapter 4.

The Frequency and Form of Supervision

The widely accepted standard for the frequency of supervision for experienced social workers is monthly (Social Work Reform Board 2010; MacDonnell 2011). For newly qualified social workers in their Assessed and Supported Year of Employment, the initial standard is weekly for six weeks and then at least fortnightly for the remainder of the first six months. These are standards you can reasonably use to prompt your supervisor and employing organization if these base standards are not met. In Chapter 5, 'When things go wrong', some ideas and potential approaches to these challenges are given.

The standard length of a supervision meeting is recognized as one and a half hours, uninterrupted. Access to advice and informal discussions with the supervisor are in addition and supplementary to this. They should not be seen as a substitute for supervision.

After the initial high intensity, early professional development and induction stages for new social workers, employers have to set a standard which is consistent with the leadership of the social work profession and national employer standards, and is a real expectation of the organization. The enduring failure of a significant proportion of social workers to receive supervision or to receive it infrequently is not acceptable. It is disturbing that it continues to be tolerated. It reflects poorly on our own sense of self-worth and professionalism.

As social workers move into more senior positions of professional authority and with **earned autonomy** (see Glossary), the focus in supervision will become even more a shared process of learning and problem solving. A frequency of every six weeks could be reasonable for a social worker in a designated senior practice role.

Appropriate and Proportionate Supervision

The form and frequency of supervision which a social worker requires vary in relation to our experience, including experience in our current role, and seniority. It may need to vary for the kind of work we do. Tsui (2005: 7) characterizes this as the 'debate between interminable supervision and autonomous practice'. While unchallenged practice, in the absence of structured, disciplined, analytic reflection and account-ability, is not acceptable, progressive and earned autonomy needs to be achieved.

The psychotherapy traditions and the reflective origins of social work expect continuing supervision, in an appropriate and propor-tionate form, throughout our career. However, the administrative tradi-tions of social welfare analysed by Tsui (2005) represent the managerialist forces which risk imposing permanent case management and performance management supervision on our profession (Chard and Ayre 2010). This is infantilizing and potentially repressive. It can lead to experienced, capable and accountable professionals being permanently treated like junior members of staff or social workers at the beginning of their career. It creates the impression that everyone is judged as requiring the same close oversight and micro-management as the least experienced or least competent.

Supervisors and leaders have to prepare social workers for earned autonomy and self-directed learning, greater trust and delegation, perhaps against the spirit of current managerial culture and national practice guidance (Jones 2004; Munro 2011). Nevertheless, accountability and the need for challenge and rigorous progressive professional development remain throughout our careers.

THE HAZARDS AND BENEFITS OF THE OPEN DOOR

All social workers will need access to advice and guidance from their manager at times between supervision sessions. This need will reduce as we become more experienced, we build our peer group for informal professional support and if the organization is more willing to trust and to delegate. There will remain the need to avoid surprises and all supervisors will welcome being advised of issues which may have wider repercussions. The supervisor's open door can be both a curse and a lifeline. While at times it is welcome and a necessity, equally, it can lead to social workers not building their own self-confidence, supervisors engendering a culture of dependency, and both not waiting and preparing well in advance for planned supervision. It may also be a good indicator of how much the whole organization is willing and able to trust social workers, becoming respected and confident professionals, allowed to make decisions.

Access to informal supervision is greatly valued. Great care needs to be taken to record key case decisions made. Informal supervision should never be an alternative to regular, booked formal supervision. It is a valuable supplement, not a substitute for supervision.

QUALITY ASSURANCE AND AUDIT BY OURSELVES AND OUR EMPLOYERS

Quality assurance of supervision is the responsibility of both the line manager of the supervisor and the senior managers and leaders responsible for social work services. Equally, as professional social workers we have individual responsibility for self-audit and for sharing the results with our workplace and across our profession.

✓ **Good Practice Checklist: Quality Assurance and Audit**

✓ Did the supervision session take place?
✓ How long did it last?
✓ Was it uninterrupted?
✓ What was the agenda?
✓ Was the agenda fully covered?
✓ Are there a supervision agreement and a personal development plan?
✓ Have they been reviewed?
✓ Do supervisors and supervisees consider that the supervision standards have been met?
✓ How is case supervision evidenced in case records?
✓ Can evidence of supervision be seen in improved service outcomes?

More subjective measurements are arguably more revealing and of greater value:

✓ Did you find the supervision helpful?
✓ Were good decisions taken on the cases discussed?
✓ Did your supervisor collate your team's development needs and ensure the professional development took place?
✓ Did it improve the service provided?

All of these are valuable for the audit. The employing organization needs to decide what critical and proportionate information is to be collected and interpreted. There should be, at least, a confidential survey for supervisors and supervisees on whether the supervision standards have been met. While a degree of confidentiality in data collection is required to encourage open reporting, it should be sufficiently team-specific to enable remedial action to be taken where non-compliance has occurred. Sampling of supervision records is valuable and economical. Care needs to be taken that the valuable confidential content can be respected, whether this relates to cases or the personal circumstances of the supervisee.

The supervision training received by the supervisors and information on refresher training need to be recorded and be at the heart of the service staff development plan. This training needs to be specific to social work and ideally validated to contribute to formal **continuing professional development** (see Glossary) and post-qualifying award modules. Supervisors and managers need just as much social work professional development as front-line staff in practice.

Senior managers are responsible for assuring the quality of supervision and the provision of skilled and effective social work services through case records. Many regularly audit small random samples of case files and supervision records to ensure adherence to policy, best practice and the provision of high quality supervision. Even if they do not, service inspections and inquiries after tragedies now routinely examine such records. They can provide evidence of good practice or indicate how problems could have been avoided. Some commercially provided electronic case records provide the facility for a manager, including the supervisor, to record a case discussion and the case-specific element of supervision on the electronic case file. This gives the opportunity for supervision to be audited at the same time as case files are audited and reviewed. This will be in addition to the supervision, accountability and oversight of their work by their line manager.

With our greater confidence within our profession, with an assertive expectation of supervision standards, and therefore owned and upheld by ourselves, there will be more self-audit. Good quality supervision will be valued and sought. There is the potential to incorporate professional development plans and records of achievements within supervision records, ready for professional re-registration. This model is both economical and self-policing.

It is necessary for us to have open exploration and analysis of the reasons behind any failure to deliver the requisite and basic standards of supervision, including evidence of shared critical analysis and reflection. This is part of the building of the **learning organization** and the development of the social worker as an assertive and confident practitioner who has a right to good professional development. It can be an antidote to the 'fractured relationship' described by Evans (2009: 145) in the observation of the relationships between social workers and their managers. It was found that where remedial work with individual supervisors and line managers was identified as necessary, the learning activities entailed focused work in small groups of peers on how they can adapt the external expectations to their own agency standards in ways that can join best practice to the work pressures which they faced each day.

ENHANCED SUPERVISION AT TIMES OF PRESSURE AND CHALLENGE

Both the social worker and their employing organization may at times come to a decision that additional close supervision, including support and enhanced professional development, is required due to particular circumstances. These could include recent critical inspections, a local serious incident, major service reorganization, surges in work pressures or concern about the social worker's personal circumstances. All of these should not make the provision of this additional supervision seem punitive or shameful. Being pro-active and providing help to support professional staff in challenging circumstances is the mark of a truly professional service and a confident profession. In addition to one-to-one supervision, the social worker should feel encouraged and helped to access external peer and expert mentoring.

The need for additional professional supervision and support will be just as acute and vital for social workers in senior roles, including management positions. Circumstances which would indicate the value of this support, indeed necessity, include critical incidents, major budget and service reductions, adverse publicity due to perceived service failure, major policy changes and the emergence of new kinds of service demand.

ADDITIONAL SUPERVISION DUE TO CONCERNS ABOUT THE WORK OF A SOCIAL WORKER

None of us want to contemplate that we may need additional support or that the quality of our work is causing concern, but it is important to be prepared and to know what you can expect. All of us need extra help at times in our work and it is important to welcome constructive help.

When a supervisor, manager or employer has any concerns about the practice or other aspects of a social worker's work, continued supervision, to the required standards, with the full range of supportive and developmental functions must be maintained. In circumstances where disciplinary action is being contemplated or an investigation is taking place, three key responsibilities need to be assumed, each assured by the supervisor:

1   Identify who is responsible for each of the tasks of any investigation and disciplinary decision-making.
2   Maintain high quality supervision, including all the key functions of assuring the quality and effectiveness of practice and the service provided, shared critical analysis and reflection, professional knowledge and skill development and accessing continuing professional development.
3   Identify with the social worker the additional 'off-line' mentoring and support they require and provide the necessary help to secure this.

It is important to avoid getting stuck on general concerns about the quality of work. It is vital to ensure any formal performance concerns are addressed in a systematic way, with a process that begins and ends. Wonnacott (2012: 148) identifies a framework for the analysis of early concerns about performance:

- organizational issues;
- quality of supervision;
- personal response to the demands of the role;
- skills and knowledge.

For each of these factors, action is required, which can be jointly agreed in supervision. This approach clearly places responsibilities on the supervisor and the employing organization, which can help free up the supervisee to play their part in any changes required, rather than feeling solely the source of the problem.

Example from Practice

Mark is a very experienced social worker who seemed to have 'peaked' in the level of his expertise and effectiveness and does not have the aptitude or skills to move into a senior practitioner or other leadership role. Nevertheless, he still has a useful part to play in a team. It will not be possible to give him as much autonomy as his experience might suggest. As his supervisor and team manager, Anne, can allocate work which is within his capabilities and when necessary undertake some supplementary and support work herself or re-allocate to another social worker. While she could not have a whole team of such people, it is a waste of members of our profession to simply discard them or not use their talents well.

SUPERVISION FOR EXPERIENCED SOCIAL WORKERS AND OTHERS

If we as professional social workers move out of direct practice into a role and with responsibilities which benefit from our professional qualification and status, we retain responsibility for our own professional development, including updating and increasing our knowledge and skills. While registration as a social worker may not be a requirement of our employer, or perhaps strictly in law; even if the post is not designated as a social worker, it is not ethical to let professional registration lapse. It would show a lack of responsibility for our obligations for leadership within our profession. It suggests a limited sense of professional identity or respect for our own professional origins. To turn our back on our profession and the responsibilities that go with it, would betray scant respect for social work colleagues and an arrogance in opting out of adherence to standards, including disciplined continuing professional development.

All of us require regular reflective supervision by a registered social worker, with the standard functions of supervision, quality assurance, shared reflection and decision-making, education and development. A minimum of booked supervision every six weeks remains advisable, with a clear and structured emphasis on all the functions of supervision. As an experienced and senior practitioner, we may show overconfidence in our knowledge and practice skills. We continue to need access to high level and challenging continuing professional development and education. There is a good range of modular post-qualifying awards provided through commissioning and partnerships with universities which can provide opportunities to enhance our professional expertise and provide enduring and externally validated evidence of our capability.

However 'settled' as an experienced social worker we may be in our present post, a regular review of our career and personal development plan continues to be valuable. Equally, our employer will wish to make the best use of our expertise and experience. We have a responsibility to provide support and consultation to our less experienced colleagues as a peer and part of our shared professional network. In return, we should continue to be supported in access to high quality professional development opportunities.

The professional supervisor of social workers in these senior and leadership positions may find a person who is 'stuck', where they are weary or the responsibilities have moved on beyond their levels of energy and enthusiasm. Without moving into formal discussion about capability, a private and 'off the record' conversation about their feelings about their role and their personal life plans can be of enormous help.

Example from Practice

Asking Helen, a very experienced and senior colleague, what she would like to be doing in the next two years opened up a positive conversation about how tired she was and how her work felt at times to have moved on beyond her own sense of competence. It was possible with the help of Human Resources to plan for retirement in about two years' time. Helen's enthusiasm was refreshed and in supervision important short-term work was arranged alongside succession planning so that arrangements were put in place for the time when she intended to retire. She returned to her 'old self', an energetic, respected and valued colleague.

Some experienced social workers may have found a 'safe haven' in their current location and be resistant to playing their full part as a senior professional. They may have been allowed to 'coast'. While respecting the degree of autonomy such social workers may have earned, the supervisor has the responsibility to challenge and encourage them to fulfil their responsibilities and make a full contribution as mature and senior professionals.

Most line managers and supervisors will at times be responsible for supervising social workers who are more experienced and capable than they are. The social worker and supervisor may each consider themselves a better and more knowledgeable practitioner than the other. Both parties must not despair. A relationship of mutual trust must be maintained with a clear and shared sense of mutual learning and **reflection** (see Glossary), coupled with clarity on accountabilities. The supervisor will have their own responsibilities to access continuing professional development and education to enhance their capability in order to be credible, useful and challenging.

Good Practice Point: Do My Job Better

Some of my own best learning as a supervisor, manager and leader has been when a member of my team has come to supervision, shut the door and told me how, and helped me, to do my job better!

DO DIFFERENT SPECIALISMS IN SOCIAL WORK REQUIRE DIFFERENT STYLES OF SUPERVISION?

Many of the current concerns about the provision of supervision for social workers have focused on social workers early in their career and in child protection. In England, later than in Wales and Northern Ireland, following the death of Victoria Climbié, the government funded a three-year pilot – for social workers in their first year after qualifying – of targetted supervision, managed workloads and professional development. In addition, special training was provided for their supervisors, which was very well regarded:

> The significance of enhanced supervision . . . the implications of this are quite profound for the future of social work. I hope so much that this will be pursued despite all the changes and difficulties which confront the profession at the present time. Much work needs to be done in this matter which in some ways represents the very heart of social work.

> (Stevenson 2010)

In fact, the level of supervision, although attracting additional government funding through the sector skills body, was regarded by employers as a reasonable minimum expectation and standard (McKitterick 2009–11).

There is a risk of lower expectations of supervision for social workers working in adult services. However, their responsibilities are of equal complexity, even if they may be masked by an emphasis on gathering information, screening and assessment as has been articulated by the Munro Review (Munro 2011) in child protection social work. In adult services, social workers are responsible for, and have particular skills in:

- the management of risk in those situations where a person is in significant danger of exploitation by those they pay to care for them;
- working with complex needs and situations of conflict or where there are differing interests;
- investigations of abuse or neglect and responsibility for the successful delivery of the collaborative work required to safeguard the individual;
- being the 'navigator' of care and support services to assist people to identify and freely choose those which they wish to use (McKitterick 2009).

These skills are particularly relevant to the current 'personalization' or self-directed support agenda in adult services. The findings of a study in this field by Beresford et al. (2011) identified choice and control and the emphasis on the relationship between the service user and the practitioner, which are core to the values and skills of social work. In both adult social care and children's services, the social worker will be working through others, in directly supervising work (see Chapter 6), co-working and providing leadership within the overall service where their professional skills will be exercised in modelling, informal mentoring and consultation.

In all fields and work settings we must be assured of the best stand-ards of supervision, including planned continuing professional develop-ment, and demand that we receive this. If this is not in place, the full contribution of our professional skills and qualification will fall into disuse. This would be a loss to the current service where we are working and more insidiously we may find ourselves unable to move back into other areas of social work.

When we work as social workers in multi-disciplinary teams, we may find that there is a tendency for the team to agree on a common and shared set of intervention skills as we share the work and build a cohesive and consensual team. The hazard or drawback of this can lead to a least skilled, undifferentiated, lowest common denominator way of working. Professional disciplines with a stronger tradition than social work of progressive professional development can be better placed to retain and articulate their particular authority and specific skills in intervention. Social workers, and in particular our social work supervisors and leaders, need to work positively and energetically to retain and develop their particular skills and evidence-based and evidence-informed practice.

HOW SUPERVISION CAN BE SUPPLEMENTED

There are a variety of supplementary sources for supervision which can be valuable, while they should not be seen as an alternative to regular planned and recorded sessions. Consultation with colleagues is a sign of an established professional peer network or a well functioning team. In these circumstances the responsibilities for the outcome remain with the social worker. Some teams encourage a formal 'buddy' system for less experienced social workers. More experienced social workers and particularly those in senior roles have a responsibility to provide advice, consultation and support. All social workers should expect to both give and seek advice from colleagues in other specialist service areas. The continuing growth in specialist roles and services can mean the allocation of cases to multiple social workers. Both formal and informal consultation and informal supervision are excellent ways of sharing and developing knowledge, rehearsing analysis and judgements, enhancing practice skills. It can reduce the unnecessary multiple allocation of single cases.

Group supervision and peer learning sets are effective ways of developing reflective and analytical skills, sharing knowledge and progressing self-directed learning as part of growing autonomy. They encourage the growth of a professional peer network to provide support, shared learning and an opportunity to present and explore one's own practice skills and knowledge. Clarity on case accountability remains key, both the accountability of the individual social worker and their accountabilities to their line manager supervisor. One great advantage of peer learning is the opportunity it gives to marshal and rehearse critical analysis and review research evidence in preparation for individual supervision, preparation of formal reports, case conferences, reviews and court.

Good Practice Box: Supplementary Forms of Supervision

- Building a peer network with colleagues at work and outside with people you trained with and friends in social work.
- Conferring with colleagues in your team.
- Seeking out opportunities for co-working with other social workers.
- 'Off-line' supervision which may be available as part of your continuing professional development or your assessed and supported year of employment (ATSE).
- Coaching, mentoring or 'buddying' arranged with your supervisor.
- Making an informal arrangement for mentoring with a more experienced, senior colleague.
- Supervision arranged for you because your line manager and supervisor is not a registered social worker.
- Using team meetings for peer supervision, sharing of research reading and other forms of group learning.

All these can be of great value, but should not be allowed to excuse your employer from their responsibility to provide good quality, reflective supervision and supporting you in your continuing professional development. They should be seen as complementary rather than remedial, rather than a reason not to provide formal supervision and access to validated progressive professional development.

MANAGING OURSELVES

The Emotional Components of Supervision

The complexity and the charged emotions of social work practice bring raw feelings and sometimes echoes of past and current emotions into the realm of our supervision. This is both an important opportunity for enhanced reflection and learning but it also brings a risk of role confusion. The skilled supervisor will be able to work out with us, as a peer, how far the personal should be discussed or exposed. The purpose of our supervision is to ensure that the focus remains on an effective service, the professional development of the social worker and overall well-being. All managers have a responsibility to assure the well-being of the people they manage, but they are not therapists for them. Just because social work supervisors could do this, they should not. If they venture too far into the personal and private lives of the social workers they supervise, they jeopardize mutual respect and esteem. The use of friends, colleagues, and external or confidential counselling should be encouraged if needed. Our supervisor is not our therapist or friend, although at times they can come close to these roles. Good supervision is usually very therapeutic, helping us in our work role, but not in our personal life.

At all times our supervisor needs to be alert to the risks of identifying us with the problems of the people using our service through a process of **transference** (see Glossary), where the emotions and the attributes of the people we serve can be unconsciously transferred over to the supervisor's perceptions of the social worker. The pressures of **managerialism** (see Glossary) and performance management are oppressive enough, without adding the burden of being identified as a client or user of services! Nevertheless the skilful supervisor can draw this kind of emotional or semi-conscious experience into the shared work with the social worker in reflection and critical analysis.

Receiving supervision in social work is not the same as receiving a social work service, there are clear distinctions and some parallels. The problems which the social worker is working with may reflect back into their relationship with their supervisor. This is part of the process of transference described by Mattinson (1975). The closeness of the social worker and their engagement with the person they are working with may cause them to be seen or identified with the problem 'out there'. We may use distancing, objectifying and disrespectful words about the service we provide for our work to show the feelings we experience when sharing the troubling and challenging problems faced by those we serve.

Social work services often provide the last resort, when other services have withdrawn or are unable to help. Social workers are often working with people who have been failed by social policy, they experience discrimination and stigma (Adams 2002).

Many people have no choice in coming to or being given a social work service. It is not one that people have 'to deserve'. I reflect on this when we apply 'eligibility criteria'. It may be that service eligibility criteria have not been met and other services may not be made available, nevertheless we have no reason not to provide a positive service in the quality of the relationship, the 'how' we relate, how we empathize and comfort, how we advise and how we help people access other services, including universal services.

The ordinary working atmosphere of pressure and demands, the restless need to be busy, are not conducive to thoughtfulness and are not emotionally healthy if not interspersed with protected time and space. Oakeshott (1989: 33) describes the crowded life where people are continually occupied and engaged but have no time to stand back and think. The Munro Review (Munro 2011: para. 6.11) adds: 'A working life given over to distracted involvement does not allow for the integration of experience.' This is, in the language of Kadushin (1976: 229): 'nourish and enhance the capacity for adaptation, alleviate psychological pain, restore emotional equilibrium, comfort, bolster and refresh', highlighting the healing and enabling role of supervision.

THE POTENTIAL IMBALANCE OF EXPERIENCE AND CAPABILITY IN SUPERVISION

The supervisor may have less social work experience than the supervisee. The supervisee may not respect their professional competence or judgement. Nonetheless the accountability remains and the supervisor retains the responsibility for assuring your professional development. Whether the supervisee feels confident enough to raise the issue or not, it will be necessary to strengthen the professional peer support system and any reasonable employer will be willing to secure additional mentor or consultation support. The supervisor may never have received good supervision themselves and need to undertake training.

The supervisee can assist by preparing well for supervision, with a clear agenda, high expectations and sharing their own knowledge and experience. The supervisee should never start by saying 'What do you want to know?' This will only encourage a managerialist and controlling session! Remember, like the new social worker, you too can re-invigorate the tired, the jaded and disengaged manager and supervisor.

PROFESSIONAL DEVELOPMENT FOR SUPERVISORS, MANAGERS AND LEADERS OF SOCIAL WORK SERVICES

The Policy Background

Many social workers who become managers have had training in practice education to prepare them for supervising students. This is a valued and appropriate preparation but cannot be seen as sufficient alone. Most employers have generic management development training for all their managers but very few indeed have any specialist training for the responsibilities, skills and knowledge required for supervising, managing and leading social workers. In adult social care the management induction standards are focused on management and administrative functions, rather than practice skills (Skills for Care 2009). All the standards could apply to management of any service, in any industry. The ten principles adopted by the General Social Care Council (2010) for the post-qualifying award in leadership and management for social workers in services for adults, children and families are, all but one, universal to any manager and leader.

The management standards the Council have set for this training and qualification are again those for general management. While the social worker undertaking this post-qualifying education has the opportunity to focus on their own professional social work skills and knowledge base, this is not required to achieve the award. It is not part of the assessment requirements. None of this devalues the qualification as a preparation for general management, but it does indicate a hollowness in our profession's infrastructure, in our capacity to prepare and support practitioners and leaders. This void is reflected in expectations at the most senior leadership level of services. For example, the National College for Leadership of Schools and Children's Services (2011) has identified five areas which cover the functional aspects of the role of the Director of Children's Services:

1   integrated service delivery;
2   partnership working;
3   managing the political and corporate context;
4   community engagement and cohesion;
5   improving outcomes for children and young people.

The first four are key roles in any public service organization, the fifth is service-specific, but silent on leadership, research knowledge and practice skills. This is not to denigrate the College or these functional areas for the most senior leaders of any human services, but it is evidence that the leadership of the social work profession and professional practice is unlikely to come from this source.

Earlier government guidance on the skills, knowledge and behaviours for leaders and those managing children's services (Department for Education and Skills 2006) was more focused on aspects of the work and included 'Nurturing team members' professional skills and insights in relation to protecting children'. This guidance should still stand for leaders and senior managers, but the five functions identified by the College suggest that most senior leaders have the focus of their work squeezed and put on a more managerialist agenda. It should remain just as important to nurture professional skills and to have insights in protecting children.

Example from Practice

My own experience of supporting employers implementing targeted supervision and professional development for newly qualified social workers and those early in their professional career has been that without the active leadership at the most senior level, improvements do not take place, despite special additional funds and access to substantial, but un-certificated training for supervisors. Equally, working in government interventions following very critical service inspections, I have found the lack of active and energetic leadership of social work practice at the most senior levels to be one of the root causes of service failure.

Gould and Baldwin (2004) refer to a study by Davies and Bynner (1999) which found that certificated learning for social work managers 'improved the quality of work produced, increased the shelf life of learning and made them more conscientious about learning'. An evaluation of a leadership and management programme, which included an assessed assignment, in services for children and families, by Brown (2011) showed significant personal and organizational changes, verified by third parties. Professional development provided in these kinds of formal and validated ways shows how real service impacts can be achieved.

Employers need to commission specialist supervision and leadership training for their social workers who are leaders and managers and to prepare social workers for these roles. This must include at its core a focus on evidence-based social work practice skills. This needs to be validated and certificated to ensure that not only learning has taken place but also to show that it has benefited and improved the service.

Good Practice Checklist: a Model for Supervision and Leadership Training

✓ Training bespoke to the needs of social work.
✓ Enhancing skills in enabling reflection and critical thinking.
✓ Learning styles and learning methods.
✓ Supervision styles and responsibilities.
✓ Accessing and using research in social work practice.
✓ Validation of training within the post-qualifying award modular framework.
✓ Provision of regular refresher training.

There are substantial benefits to using external validation of training and education.

Social workers who are supervisors of social workers in practice and students should have formal specialist education in social work supervision, validated and refreshed every three years, with a particular focus on continuing to develop their own professional knowledge and practice base. The content of training must include current practice and policy issues, research evidence, both focused on their own specialist service area, and include wider learning across interrelated and other fields of social work services.

The place of **post-qualifying awards** (see Glossary) with partner universities can be key to the training and professional development of social work leaders and supervisors. The external validation gives quality assurance, ensuring local, internal practice is good, leadership standards and expectations are high, and provides the opportunity for objective assessment against national standards. It strengthens the links between practice and academic learning and research and helps share expertise and good practice across social work employers. Critically for us as social workers, these awards give credible, enduring and progressive evidence of our professional practice knowledge and skills. Modular post-qualifying awards, commissioned by employers, with capability and practice skills development objectively assessed and validated give discipline and portable evidence. Employers and universities who have invested in collaborative, multi-agency partnerships have shown how practice-based and academically validated post-qualifying training is fit for purpose and affordable.

The Position and Experience of First Line Managers of Social Workers

Team managers in both services for adults and children and families have a challenging and vital role within their service. They arguably have the most pressured role, accountable to the public for the work of their whole team, and with the whole of their own organization on top of them. They are responsible for screening all new work, resource allocation, quality assurance of assessments and plans of intervention, specific case decision-making, working with a wide range of external agencies and professionals, meeting specific performance targets, the professional supervision of their staff, co-working and deputizing for them. This is a mix of the general management responsibilities of any first line manager and the professional development, leadership, coaching and mentoring of social workers, coupled with significant case responsibilities. Undoubtedly the management and leadership skills identified by GSCC (2010) are important for first line managers and supervisors of social workers, however, without substantial expansion, this is not sufficient for the full range of skills, knowledge and expertise required in services for adults, families and children.

The Joint Area Review of Haringey Children's Services (Ofsted 2008) found: 'There is insufficient evidence of managerial oversight and decision-making on case records in children's social care services . . . There is also limited evidence of thorough analytical and reflective supervision to ensure individual casework is carried out effectively.' Inspectors expect to see evidence on case files in both the recording by the social worker and their supervisor of how they have come to decisions.

This expectation brings us back to the core of good supervision, placing reflective supervision at the heart of the management function described above. It identifies the vital nature of this activity and the discharge of this responsibility as central and critical to the delivery of safeguarding of children and for effective family support. Exactly the same is applicable in the adult social work specialisms, where there is the same focus on effective intervention and meeting complex needs.

The professional relationship within supervision places strong mutual responsibilities for preparing for supervision which is the subject of Chapter 4. An organization providing a good social work service will have the key elements of supervision policies and procedures embedded, owned and led by the senior managers and leaders as part of their individual professional social work standards and identities. Supervisors, managers and leaders all have responsibilities to ensure their own practice skills are as required for their different roles. This has to be coupled with knowledge of current research as part of their own continuing professional development. Reflection and critical analysis are as vital to the way they work as they are to any other member of the profession. The most senior and experienced social workers are well placed to openly demonstrate and model how they are continuing in their own professional development.

4 Preparing for supervision

Key to getting the best out of supervision is preparation. Part of this is the organization putting the basic resources in place, having high expectations and respecting its importance. Supervisors need training and regular refresher courses. All social workers need access to progressive professional development opportunities which are specific to social work. Supervision is not just an appointment in the diary which comes round at regular intervals. Both we as the social worker and as the supervisor have to prepare for it. As the social worker, we can help our supervisor give us good supervision, and as the supervisor we can be far more effective and helpful if we do work beforehand too.

✓ **Good Practice Checklist:**
Supervisee, be Prepared

✓ Be prepared and have your agenda ready.
✓ Be clear on what you want and need from the supervision session.
✓ Take control of the agenda.
✓ Know what particular performance indicators are important for your supervisor and the organization, identify what part you contribute to them and ask for any assistance you need to help meet these.
✓ Address a small part of your caseload for critical analysis and reflection, focusing on what you are doing, or wish to do, to achieve positive change.

✓ Make it interesting and exciting for your supervisor, give them some professional inspiration.
✓ Consider bringing some relevant research or other reading to stimulate the session.
✓ Check your individual **continuing professional development** plan (see Glossary) is being addressed.
✓ Open your diary at the end of the session to confirm the next date and time for supervision.

Professional supervision does not just happen, it is not just a one-to-one meeting between a staff member and their line manager. The focus and rigour, as has been identified in earlier chapters, are critical to good, safe and effective services.

Social work is a graduate profession with post-qualifying training and development set at first or master's degree levels. Both the supervisee and supervisor need to bring their own qualities of 'graduateness' with them. What is 'graduateness'?

Recently Ross (2011) provided a definition of the qualities of graduates:

Honours graduates will have detailed knowledge, some of it at the forefront of current research; they will be able to deploy established techniques of analysis and enquiry; they will be able to devise and sustain arguments and to solve problems; they will be able to comment on current research; they will appreciate the uncertainty, ambiguity and limits of knowledge; they will be able to manage their own learning, using scholarly reviews and primary sources; they will be able to extend their knowledge independently and initiate and carry out projects; they will be able to critically evaluate arguments, assumptions and abstract concepts, and frame appropriate questions for solving problems, and communicate to specialist and non-specialist audiences.

In the nineteenth century the academic theologian Newman (1852) used ambitious language for the qualities of graduates,

> "To see things as they are, to go right to the point, to disentangle a skein of thought, to fill any post with credit, and to master any subject with facility . . . to accommodate himself to others, how to throw himself into their state of mind, how to bring before them his, how to influence them, how to come to an understanding with them, how to bear with them."

This enthusiastic language is an inspiring reminder of our abilities and responsibilities, although of course the gender specific words are wrong!

These qualities and expectations should form the basis of the mutual respect and intellectual rigour of supervision. If supervision only consists of administrative checks on performance indicators, the opportunity is being lost of utilizing the combined abilities of both participants.

PREPARATION BY THE EMPLOYING ORGANIZATION AND SENIOR LEADERS

A clear and specific policy for the provision of professional supervision for social workers and the audit and quality assurance of its delivery are the foundations of good services. This requires active leadership, closely overseen and nurtured, if not directly led, at director level. The neglect of supervision will be identified in negative service inspections and in inquiries after tragedies and service failures. My own direct experience in government interventions in 'failing' services indicates that the lack of rigorous and positive supervision, especially for newer social workers, is an early and reliable predictor of service failure.

The organization needs to foster a culture of learning and respect for thoughtful reflection. The 'sacred space' for supervision has been referred to earlier. This requires a private room, respect for appointments for supervision and protection for planned professional development activities. Some employers have initiated 'hot desking' for staff. Are private rooms easily available? Sometimes supervision takes place in open plan offices or cafés, but this is not acceptable. It devalues the activity and puts confidentiality and trust at risk. Social workers need to know that senior managers expect them to receive regular good quality supervision. The need for supervision training, regularly refreshed and updated, has been referred to earlier.

The leaders and senior managers themselves should provide a model of how they ensure they receive their own professional supervision, be it through a mentor, peer review, structured continuing professional development or other means. If they show how they need and value this, they will provide a model and incentive for everyone else to follow and emulate.

The 'Hard' Resources

The 'hard' resources required are secured in policies, finance and formal systems, and include an ambitious supervision policy, regularly reviewed, audit and quality assurance, respect for assured uninterrupted planned time, quiet, private rooms, time and financial resources for continuing professional development, including specifically for supervisors. Training programmes for social workers need to include both the inter-professional and inter-disciplinary provision for all staff, and training specific for the development of their social work intervention skills. The latter is often totally ignored.

Partnerships with universities, actively led at the most senior level, are vital in fostering and accessing research in social work practice, with shared arrangements for modular post-qualifying awards. These will provide shared and objective evaluation of learning and skills development with enduring recognition of continuing professional development. The provision of service or team libraries, coupled with access to electronic research sources and access arrangements to partnership universities libraries (see Chapter 7) is needed.

The provision of professional learning and development of social workers should not be dependent on special government funding. Most other professions within local government do not wait for government initiatives to secure their development and professionalism.

The 'Soft' Resources

The 'soft' resources are of equal value and can be as hard to secure and sustain. The term '*learning organization*' is well known and well used, but not always easy to achieve. It is cultural, it needs to be led by the most senior figures and leaders outwards across the whole organization, focusing on the value of constantly addressing how the services can be continuously improved by learning, evaluating new ways of working and investing in the skills and ambitions of all staff. In many organizations, including a substantial proportion of local authorities, the learning and development function is located outside the service department. While this can bring organizational efficiencies, including an easier corporate focus, it hinders embedding cohesive and internal ownership of the professional development of social workers, including those in management and other senior roles, within the service.

This is especially relevant for first line managers of social workers, who with all their many conflicting responsibilities, can see the organizational distancing of staff development as a release from responsibility for their professional development. In addition, the same centralized corporate staff development function will regard them as general managers first and foremost, and will focus on this aspect of their work. These first line managers are fundamental to the social work profession in its leadership, professional development and the provision of evidence-based practice. In the first two years of the Department for Education pilot programmes for newly qualified social workers, which included targeted funding for staff release for supervision, managed case loads and professional development, the first line managers remained the least committed to the pilots, despite specialist supervision training for them

(McKitterick 2009–11). The reasons given were the pressure of work and an unreasonable expectation that newly qualified social workers could 'hit the ground running'. However, there was no correlation with the relative demands for services in the areas served.

In the current target-driven culture of managerialism (Chard and Ayre 2010), the load on first line managers, in terms of work volume, complexity and diversity, requires sustained attention in the building of a healthy and supportive culture for social work services. The leaders have a key role in the leadership and role modelling for social workers. Some organizations have experimented with devolving some of the developmental aspects of supervision within the team to senior colleagues or for social workers early in their careers to practise being educators and mentors. This is a valuable area of development but rarely releases line managers from case and service accountability. Consequently, the responsibilities for both reflective supervision on individual cases where they are accountable, and assurance of continuing professional development remain.

Fostering and maintaining a culture and working atmosphere of efficient, thoughtful working, with work pressures managed to protect the sacred space required for reflective supervision, calm deliberation with colleagues and dedicated and protected time for planned professional development can be hard work in many service settings. It can be counter to the prevailing culture. The excitement of demanding services, crises and heavy workloads can become habitual, if not moderately addictive. The adrenalin rush of a crisis or a busy office can take over as the impetus for work. 'Busy-itis' is one term used. I know of no other profession whose members allow their professional development to be so easily shunted aside or cancelled due to work pressure. The question is, is it an indication of lack of self-worth, a lack of interest and commitment to our own professional development, or the denial by employing organizations of the value in investing in the enhancement in the skills and effectiveness of their own staff? I suspect it is a combination of all three.

Good Practice Checklist: Professional Development and Support of Social Workers

A culture that fosters and promotes the professional development of social workers must show the following features:

✓ Encourage active membership of professional social work bodies.

✓ Support social workers, however senior or early in their career, to contribute to the development of social work policies and presentations of successful innovative work both locally and nationally. This recognizes the benefits for the local service in terms of repute and access to learning from others.

✓ Ensure that all senior staff who are social workers retain their registration and openly join colleagues in internal and external continuing professional development activities to retain registration.

✓ Link the organization's policy for continuing professional development with that on supervision.

✓ Align career progression and job roles to the national professional capabilities framework and the modular post-qualifying awards with partner universities.

✓ Senior members of the profession, both leaders and senior managers, model the pursuit of continuing professional development and accountability for progressive knowledge and practice skills development, including research awareness.

In order for supervision to be successful for both parties, and contribute to the development of a good working environment, space and respect for supervision and professional development have to be created. Respect for supervision is key to its inclusion on the agenda of the organization.

Good Practice Checklist: Creating Space and Respect

✓ Working with colleagues to provide mutual cover for these activities.

✓ Commitments at recruitment and induction to provide high quality supervision and individual, regularly reviewed, professional development plans. This will support successful recruitment and retention.

✓ Formal supervision agreements which specify frequency and professional development activities.

✓ Demonstrating the success to the employing organization of high quality and protected supervision in terms of outcomes, performance, service quality, recruitment and retention.

✓ Openly owning and promoting the role of the supervisor as a professional social worker, in addition to, and of equal importance to, their role and identity as the manager.

✓ Working within the work team on peer learning, shared development activities and use of research and knowledge databases.

✓ Welcoming the citation of research on evidence-informed practice in social work records and reports.

PREPARATION BY SUPERVISORS AND SOCIAL WORKERS

The Supervisor

Management of time and prioritization of tasks are basic skills for all managers and should be part of the self-management of mature professionals. The line managers could develop a time diary to analyse the tasks and distractions which are 'squeezing' supervision time out or pushing it down the scale of priorities. This will provide vital material for their own professional supervision. It should help focus the tasks, time taken and purpose of the tasks undertaken, identifying work which could be completed by others, including routine administrative tasks, potential inefficient working methods, patterns of distractions and the potential to organize and group activities to complete in a more ordered and less piecemeal way. The judgement of the relative importance of tasks and developing more efficient and effective ways of working require knowledge of what works in social work practice.

Terms like 'front line services', 'heavy end work', 'bombardment, 'the coal face' and 'operational services' are often used to describe the environment in which social workers are working. These terms are arguably derogatory and disrespectful to the people and carers served but nevertheless reflect the working experience of the workers and their managers. The danger is that the demands of the work and inevitable peaks of activity can become enervating, to the detriment of thoughtful, reflective and **critical analysis** (see Glossary).

The administrative aspects of supervision associated with performance and compliance can squeeze out the educative and supportive aspects. Participants in the study by Jones (2004) reported the use of external consultants, peer supervision and the use of learning networks. All of these are important complementary resources in the building and maintenance of our professional identity and development. The risk is that they become remedial and do not address the failure to provide professional supervision at the core of a social work service.

Good Practice Checklist: Preparation by the Supervisor

✓ Ensure the room, the time, the sacred space, will be private and undisturbed.

✓ Check the layout of the room is right, chairs of equal height and comfort, no separating desk.

✓ Be wholly focused on the task, clear your mind of other preoccupations.

✓ Be clear what you want to gain from the session and what you are going to give.

✓ Advise the social worker in advance of any particular cases or issues you want to address.

✓ Ensure you are confident in your own knowledge of current research of effective practice and current practice guidance related to the current work of the supervisee.

✓ Check you have shared the record of the last supervision with the social worker beforehand and that you have completed the tasks allocated to you.

✓ Be clear what resources and opportunities you have secured for the continuing professional development of the social worker.

✓ Read any relevant paper or electronic case records or performance data beforehand.

Example from Practice

My GP has a gap of several minutes between seeing each patient. When her patients come in, her computer screen is turned away so that she cannot be distracted by it. She only turns it to face her at the end of the consultation. She has done her preparatory work beforehand, she does not need to double check her performance targets or instructions on how to treat me. I have observed scores of social work supervision sessions when the supervisor has more eye contact with their computer screen than with the social worker!

The Social Worker

In advance of a supervision session, you should prepare to review your own continuing professional development, your own interests and ambitions for further learning. Identify any resources from your employer which are required for this, both in time and money.

Good Practice Checklist: Preparation by the Social Worker

✓ Have I reviewed my workload and identified those cases and issues I wish to discuss?

✓ For these, am I seeking the opportunity to critically analyse and reflect, and explore options for future action? Is it not possible to see a way forward?

✓ What decisions need to be taken during supervision?

✓ Are there reports or case files I would like my supervisor to read in preparation for the session?

✓ Is my workload reasonable, does it need adjustment or do I need help in setting priorities?

✓ Is the mix of my workload reasonable, appropriate for my experience and supporting my professional development?

✓ Are there performance indicators for my work and am I up-to-date with current performance data and know where the challenges lie?

✓ What action do I want my supervisor to take to make my work more successful and/or less stressful?

✓ Are there situations or events I need to share with my supervisor, so that there are no surprises?

SUPERVISION THROUGHOUT OUR CAREER

The key functions we need from our supervision are constant throughout our careers:

■ assuring the quality and effectiveness of our practice and the service we provide;

- shared critical analysis and reflection on work with individual cases and the wider service we provide;
- professional knowledge and skill development;
- planning and reviewing our continuing professional development.

We all as social workers share the need for supervision, but in varying forms of delivery and recognizing the degree of **earned autonomy** (see Glossary) that goes with our particular roles. The different forms which supervision takes change and evolve with experience, seniority and role. No social worker in direct practice, however experienced or senior, can afford not to have supervision. The same applies to all managers and leaders of social work services and equally for all engaged in teaching and research. To fail to receive it, to fail to seek it out, is not a sign of independence and competence, it is a sign of professional stagnation and complacency. The British Association of Social Workers (2011) state:

> Social Workers should take responsibility for ensuring they have access to professional supervision and discussion which supports them to reflect and make sound professional judgements based on good practice.

It is useful to look at the changing needs and evolution of styles of supervision as our experience and roles develop. The functions remain the same, how it is delivered and received will evolve and develop. It is useful to look at the form of supervision in different roles and stages in our professional journey:

- the transition from student to beginning social worker;
- the beginning social worker;
- moving from early professional development to becoming an experienced 'seasoned' social worker and senior practitioner;
- practice educators, university teachers and researchers;
- first line managers of social workers;
- senior leaders and managers of social work services.

The Transition from Student to Beginning Social Worker

In order to prepare for our career or journey of informed and improving practice we need to develop both our ability and capacity in both practice and in our learning skills. At university, the focus has been on learning, understanding and demonstrating competence in a formal assessment framework. Once in our first job, our accountabilities are to the employing organization, the people to whom we provide a social work service and to the professional registering body. We lose the fellowship and support of our fellow students and teachers. The university course had a beginning middle and an end; once qualified, our career stretches out before us, uncertain, uncharted and with no end in sight.

It is important to recognize that we learn in different ways in both supervision and other professional development activities. All our learning and professional development must include:

1 reflection and critical analysis;
2 gaining knowledge, including the ability to evaluate research on what works, being research-literate and research-aware;
3 developing the ability to process complex information and knowledge, to cogently analyse, to express the 'what' and the 'how' of our work in written and verbal communication;
4 developing our skills in our relationships and interventions as a social worker, to achieve change.

We need to check and regularly review the balance between all four. The current emphasis on **reflection** (see Glossary) in much social work education literature may exacerbate real and widespread deficits in points 2, 3 and 4. In principle, reflective learning should be the glue creating a social worker who is a continuing learner in terms of skills and knowledge. How does the reflective social worker move to conclusions and to action? How do we guard against analysis paralysis? Evaluation of knowledge and critical analysis are the traditional expectations of **graduateness** (see Glossary). Point 4 is the stuff of social work practice. It is not the process of assessment *per se* or the three tasks of care/**case management**: assessment, arranging services, and review (see Glossary).

The lack of focus within the profession on the responsibility of social workers to achieve change by their own direct intervention through a range of advocacy, therapy, relationship-based work or community action feeds a reticence in articulating and identified practice skills and methods of working. At the start of your professional career, it is vital to develop your own 'toolbox' of different social work methods and ways of working. This will help you to avoid slipping into a passive role of assessing for others to make decisions, or performing case management for others to determine whether services can be provided. As the social worker with an individual, a carer or a family, *you* are the instrument of change, their source of direct help.

Supervision needs to be used alongside other ways of learning, including reading, peer support as well as the more formal professional development identified with your supervisor. Keep reading the books, journals and accessing the knowledge websites.

The transition from university to your first job as a social worker is described by Donnellan and Jack (2010: 35):

You will no longer:

- be answerable to the academic world of your tutors, teachers or the university;
- have the ready support of a group of students, all facing similar problems together;
- be finishing your placement in a few weeks.

In taking on qualified social worker status you will:

- have duties and responsibilities defined by the policies and procedures of your employer;
- carry a corporate identity;

- be carrying full case responsibility;
- be personally accountable for your decisions and actions.

The joy at achieving your professional qualification is tempered by the shock of these changes. Supervision, the development arrangements for your first year of the assessed and supported year of employment, and the building of a new peer network are vital to establishing your confidence and growing autonomy.

The Beginning Social Worker

At the outset of our career as social workers we have much to share from our experience and knowledge gained as a student in training. If good professional supervision has been part of practice learning, then reflection, critical analysis and active consideration of current research knowledge relevant to the field in which we are now working will be part of our social work toolbox. They are good habits to hold onto and to build upon. The supervisor may be busy, distracted or just tired, the new enthusiastic social worker is a bonus in their energy, keenness to learn and vigour.

There will be specific areas of knowledge and practice experience which will not have been covered in professional training, due to gaps in the university curriculum, choices of options and practice learning opportunities. This could include, for example, the impact of dementia, parental mental illness, communicating with children, or human growth and development. 'There is no general expectation that all students undergoing generic training will develop communication skills with children, ... despite the fact that all social workers, including those who work primarily with adults, have direct contact with children' (Luckock et al. 2006: 4).

There should be no embarrassment about not knowing things, if in doubt, ask, and in preparation for supervision, identify where you think the gaps are and prepare your own ideas for how these can be filled.

Good Practice Checklist: Preparation for Personal Development Plan and Supervision Agreement

✓ Review your student practice learning opportunities and knowledge gained with the specific service area where you are now working.

✓ Identify your gaps in knowledge and experience, in terms of practice skills and methods, overall knowledge of the service, policies and procedures, relevant legislation and research.

✓ Consider how any experience before your social work training may be relevant, remembering you are now a social worker and cannot slip back to how you have worked before.

✓ Your particular interests and enthusiasms should be maintained and potential new ones identified. These will help you and your supervisor to make good use of your talents within the team and service, and contribute to the basis of your planned continuing professional development.

✓ Ask for the organization's policies and procedures on supervision, continuing professional development, annual appraisal or review and information on the arrangements for the Assessed and Supported Year of Employment (ASYE).

✓ Remember you are new, so you are allowed to ask basic questions about anything you are unsure about. No one can expect you to know everything.

✓ Remember gaps in knowledge and experience are areas for development, not something to feel awkward about.

Any development required to remedy any gaps in knowledge and experience will need to be included in the initial development plan and supervision agreement. It will be helpful to select cases which give learning opportunities, arrange opportunities to observe practice in other specialist teams and to co-work with experienced colleagues.

Those who have already worked in the service or a similar setting will have the benefit of familiarity with the working practices and some confidence in practising in this setting. Those who do not have this experience will be less confident and are likely to take time to become familiar with the work and working environment. Nevertheless it is notable how after a few months these less experienced social workers are often the more able, perhaps because they know they have had much to learn or bring new ideas and fresh approaches.

Both groups of new social workers face challenges, but often different ones. Social workers who have come to professional training from within the service can find it hard to take on the professional mantle of a different role, responsibilities and use of new practice knowledge. They may need to work hard to demonstrate to colleagues that they are now different. Equally they may have to concentrate on new ways of working, rather than relying on their previous experience. Social workers new to the service need to retain a degree of objectivity and constructive quiet criticism and challenge. They need to avoid joining any dysfunctional cultural behaviour or being overawed by the complexity and new culture they are joining. The most mature teams welcome the arrival of new social workers for the refreshment they bring, their awareness of current research and new ideas.

Qualifying as a social worker is not just getting the certificate, it is a major change in the way of working and in accountability. It is the passport to access the journey of lifelong professional development and learning, it is not a ticket for life.

Experienced 'Seasoned' Social Workers and Senior Practitioners

The qualities of self-reliance, self-support, self-education and self-criticism are all gained with experience, exacting professional development and the development of a professional peer network. The functions of supervision remain the same with growing and earned autonomy. Our accountability for effective practice is to the public and the people we serve, as much as to the employing organization. Our growing autonomy runs alongside accountability. It requires a continuing willingness to learn, to give account of how our practice is of quality and is informed by good research evidence. There are particular risks of relying on intuition and experience which can only be addressed by willing participation in reflection and sharing analysis in supervision. Intuition and experience are invaluable, but only when explicitly understood and the evidence base is articulated. With experience comes the ability to identify what areas of work the supervisee wishes to explore in supervision and where decisions need to be made in that setting. Growing professional autonomy can be demonstrated through having reviewed performance information before the supervision session and being ready to address any issues which require assistance from the supervisor.

I would include in this group social workers holding senior roles such as chairs of panels, case conferences and reviews, who exercise professional judgement and are responsible for a wide range of practice decisions. They are also in key leadership roles which can easily not be recognized or acknowledged as such. Retention of the mainstay of professional and exacting supervision for themselves is central to the effective exercise of their responsibilities.

Continuing professional development remains essential. Supervision should be used to identify and secure the means to achieve this. The regular review of development gives the opportunity to plan the next career stages, in terms of widening experience and greater specialist expertise. There is a growing responsibility as a senior professional to work with the supervisor on how best to contribute to the wider service and to the development of more junior colleagues.

The Practice Educator, University Teacher and Researcher

This group covers a wide range of roles, all important ones for the development of effective social work practice, but often not combined with direct social work practice or located within social work services. There is not the same requirement for casework accountability, but with this goes the very real challenge of retaining familiarity with current practice and service demands. Ideally, regular periods returning to practice should be arranged and social work employers will be keen to assist. One of the real dangers is that the gap between education and learning and practice widens, with a lack of mutual respect. This gap can be destructive, with the different responsibilities articulated in simplified language of academic versus the real world and unsafe and unskilled practice versus theory and evidence. The reality is that both need to be closely integrated and have shared responsibilities in growing the quality and effectiveness of social work services. The perceived differences have not been helped by the abolition of the formal partnerships of employers and universities required for social work education with the new social work degree and postgraduate qualification. These are now being rebuilt, but the investment and commitment of senior managers and leaders will be required to re-build the bridges over this gap.

Practice educators need to be kept at the centre of service delivery and not located in separate structures. The understanding of the two worlds is greatly helped by research such as that by White (2008) who uses discourse analysis and research based on ethnographic methods to get under the skin of busy social work services. The Munro Review (Munro 2011) shows how a leading academic figure can strike at the heart of the almost intolerable pressures in social work services and make authoritative recommendations for change.

Social work educators and researchers need to use the facility of supervision to retain and develop their practice skills and knowledge, plan and review their own professional development as social workers, as part of their current roles. Independent practice educators will need to secure their own supervision and be able to show both the practice settings where they work and the universities how this is being achieved and how the quality of their work is assured.

First Line Managers and Other Supervisors of Social Workers in Practice

A team manager or first line manager role is one of the toughest in the profession. They provide the still and the calm when social workers come back into the office. The employer probably wants them simply to be a general manager and piles on other responsibilities. In return for their challenging role, they deserve excellent, challenging supervision and access to the very best professional development, research sources and opportunities to learn from outside the service, with a strong peer network.

Ofsted (2012) found:

> Team Managers across many local authorities were strongly committed to ensuring that their teams' learning needs were met but were less vocal about their own needs. Those managers who had access to tailored academically accredited training that was rooted in management practice and delivered through action learning sets were most able to clearly describe the impact on their management of performance and practice.

Has recent training been received in social work supervision? Has the supervisor received good supervision? The training need can be remedied and the skills of good supervision learned and their own line manager can provide a good model, if they themselves own the discipline and benefits of reflective supervision.

The agenda for supervision is essentially the same as it is for the social worker. It remains:

- identifying any key case or service decisions which need to be jointly made or made by the manager;
- reviewing key performance issues;
- stating how the supervisor will help identify and review professional development needs and how they are being met.

The same discipline applies:

- shared critical analysis;
- mutual reflection;
- evaluation and application of relevant research.

Good Practice Checklist: Questions for Supervisors and First Line Managers

✓ Have I reviewed my workload and identified those cases, performance measures, resources and service issues I wish to discuss?

✓ For these, am I seeking the opportunity to critically analyse and reflect, and explore options for future action? Is it not possible to see a way forward?

✓ What decisions need to be taken during supervision?

✓ Are there reports or case files I would like my supervisor to read in preparation for the session?

✓ Is my workload and that of my team reasonable, does it need adjustment or do I need help in setting priorities?

✓ Is the mix of my workload reasonable, appropriate for my experience and supportive of my professional development?

✓ Reviewing the relevant performance indicators for my work, am I up to date with current performance data and know where the challenges lie?

✓ What action do I want my supervisor to take to make my work more successful and/or less stressful?

✓ Are there situations or events I need to share with my supervisor, so that there are no surprises?

✓ How can I review the continuing professional development needs of my team and identify the resources needed to meet these?

✓ Reviewing my own continuing professional development, including skills and knowledge in practice, supervision, leadership and management, my own interests and ambitions for further learning, how can I identify any resources from my employer which are required for this, in both time and cost?

PREPARATION BY SENIOR LEADERS AND MANAGERS OF SOCIAL WORK SERVICES

The Munro Review (Munro 2011: para. 7.11) commends a service where 'all managers and leaders are actively and frequently involved in a mix of case consultation, direct work with children and families and the teaching of theory and practice'. We have some way to go! Ofsted (2012: 7) identified some features in services which supported their staff effectively 'systematic performance audits and evaluation of the quality of practice and supervision'. In addition, they also highlighted 'leadership from visible and active senior managers who modelled the required behaviours' (2012: 14). It is interesting how in social work we use the term management as a catch-all for the activities of leadership, performance management, professional consultation and supervision and the making of key social work case decisions. It is important to distinguish between these different activities in order to be clear where the respective responsibilities lie. While we are building professional confidence and encouraging growing autonomy in professional social work across the employing organizations, straight line management, oversight, command, control and performance management will not build competence or creativity.

A balance of time and attention has to be maintained in supervision with the line manager addressing general management and service development issues and their own needs as a social worker who continues to learn and to demonstrate accountable practice and decision-making. This has to be a prime focus, along with developing modelling and leadership behaviour. The manager may not be a social worker and may even have no interest in the quality of the service for which the supervisee is responsible beyond reputation management, performance indicators and political expediency. In all these circumstances the supervisee needs to secure supervision, peer support, critical friends and be able to account for how they are assuring their own professional competence, retaining and progressing their own skills and knowledge. Whether or not the manager seems interested, it is important and developmental for them, to demonstrate how the supervisee, as a professional social worker is achieving all of this. No professional in public services is fully autonomous or should seek to be so.

SUMMARY

Good Practice Checklist: Preparing for Supervision, for Both the Supervisor and the Supervisee

✓ Prepare your agenda of the issues and specific practice issues you want to cover.
✓ Bring ideas, including research evidence, to use in the reflective discussion and critical analysis you plan for the session.
✓ Check your record of the last supervision session for actions agreed.
✓ Review any performance indicators beforehand to help avoid them dominating the session.
✓ Be ready with suggestions and practical steps to ensure continuing professional development is addressed.
✓ Ensure the appointed time is secure in your diary and that you have made arrangements for cover and for messages to be taken.
✓ Prepare two mugs of coffee or refreshment of your choice (some supervisors have chocolate biscuits and 'Rescue Remedy' in their desk drawer!) and take a deep breath.

5 When things go wrong

Nothing will ever be plain sailing, challenge is normal and healthy. The first thing is to make sure supervision happens and the second thing is to have an agreed agenda that is completed. When supervision is not being given or is not working for you, it is helpful to consider the reasons for this, whether you are the supervisor or the supervisee. The problems are not impossible, even if at times you may feel you are making all the effort in the partnership. It is crucial that you hold onto the ideals and models of good supervision set out in the earlier chapters. It is your professional development which is at stake as well as the quality of social work service which you provide. It can be helpful for both the supervisee and the supervisor to remind one another that, as fellow professionals, you should each uphold and adhere to your own profession's standards.

WHY IS SUPERVISION NOT CONSISTENTLY PROVIDED?

In Chapter 2, we mentioned studies that show supervision is not being consistently provided. The reasons for this are:

- Supervision is challenging, even the best friend who may be a 'critical friend' is not always welcome and is avoided.
- A busy and challenging work setting can devalue, or even openly denigrate, time set aside for careful thought and reflection.
- As social workers who want to be seen, or see ourselves as a confident, competent, independent practitioners we may wish to avoid accountability and challenge.

- We may consider that we have no further development needs that we cannot meet ourselves, we may think we have nothing more to learn.
- At times we may feel so jaded and disillusioned that we do not want to think about what we are doing.
- Our supervisor can be too busy or too disorganized to prioritize time and space for supervision.
- Our supervisor may not have had the necessary training and preparation to give good supervision; they may never have received good supervision themselves.
- We may not value or respect the skills and expertise of the supervisor.
- We may be avoiding supervision because we fear being challenged about work not done.
- We and our supervisee may have had recent informal discussions about particular cases which we see as an adequate alternative.
- Our supervisor may be on leave or their post may be vacant and the organization has failed to provide adequate cover.

Both we and our supervisor need to consider which of these reasons may apply and have an open discussion about this. Without identifying the problems, no solutions are possible. It is important to remember that supervision is a two-way relationship of shared learning, what Donnellan and Jack (2010: 138) describe as 'the supervisory alliance'.

In addition, there is within social work an undercurrent which rejects professionalism, the ownership of specific practice skills and any need to be informed by knowledge, research or consideration of effectiveness. This leads to resistance to **continuing professional development** (see Glossary) and learning from research in practice. This in turn leads on to a consequent lack of respect from people outside the profession.

Features of bad practice in supervision are:

- There is no supervision agreement.
- The session starts late.
- There are interruptions at the door or on the phone.

■ There is no agenda or planning of how the time is to be best used at the start.
■ The supervisor asks to discuss cases without having forewarned the supervisee.
■ The supervisor has not reviewed performance information they wish to discuss before the session and spends time reading off a computer screen.
■ The supervisor has not read any case records beforehand that they wish to discuss.
■ The social worker has not checked what was agreed last time for this session.
■ The social worker has not planned what they need from the session or shared it with the supervisor at the start.
■ The discussion is purely action-focused with no shared reflective discussion.
■ Research in practice and policy development are never discussed or considered.
■ No time is set aside to identify and review development needs and to arrange continuing professional development, including career planning.
■ There is no clarity on critical decisions taken or record made.
■ The supervisor does not provide a shared record of the session.
■ No date and time are set for the next session.
■ The social worker leaves uncertain of what they need to do next, feels unsupported and with their professional needs and aspirations unmet.

Features of good practice in supervision are:

■ There is a supervision agreement which reviewed regularly.
■ The session starts and finishes on time and there are no interruptions.
■ The room is quiet and private.
■ There is an agenda planned and agreed at the start which is completed to time.

- The supervisor has identified the issues they would like to discuss beforehand, and read any relevant case records and reviewed performance and management data before the session.
- Both the supervisor and the social worker have checked the record of the last session to ensure any agreed action has been taken.
- The social worker has planned what they wish to gain from the session and shared this at the beginning.
- The session covers a balance of reviewing workload, a sample of the caseload, shared critical reflection on individual cases and overall service delivery, critical case decisions which are recorded, with clarity on those which are made by the social worker, those which are shared and those made by the supervisor, planning and reviewing development needs and continuing professional development, including career planning.
- Relevant research in practice and policy developments are regularly shared and discussed.
- The supervisor provides a shared record of the session.
- The date and time of the next meeting are set for the next session.
- The social worker leaves the room knowing what is expected of them and feeling empowered to continue in their work.
- The social worker is clear on how their professional development is being assured.
- The social worker has a clear sense of their career for the immediate future.

WHAT TO DO WHEN THINGS GO WRONG

The Social Worker

- Remember it is legitimate and part of your professional responsibility to ask for the supervision policy as a basic part of your toolkit needed to do the job.

- Offer to contribute to the revision of the current policy if it needs to be updated or needs to address the specific needs of social workers.
- Share ideas from this book and examples from colleagues who work in organizations which do have a supervision policy.
- Remember banging on about your need and entitlement to good, reflective supervision from a registered social worker is part of what it means to be a professional.
- Without it you cannot be expected to provide a safe and effective service.

The first rule for us as a social worker early in our career is not to blame ourselves. While social work is rewarding, it is also challenging and personally demanding.

It is vital to develop and sustain a peer network, both within our team and in other service areas. These colleagues, along with trusted friends, give the opportunity to mull over what the problems are for us and how they could be addressed. This is not simply grumbling about our boss or the organization, they are professional discussions about how we can be well supported and our professional development assured.

We should have a supervision agreement and shared written records of our supervision. These should be regularly reviewed, along with our personal development plan and the post-qualifying training and development we have received.

We should check the delivery of our supervision against the employer standards for supervision with our supervisor. If these are not specific to social work, check what you have been receiving against national standards, for example, the British Association of Social Workers College of Social Work policy (MacDonnell 2011) and the Social Work Reform Board (2011) *Standards for Employers and Supervision Framework*. You can prepare and rehearse your concerns and suggestions for a resolution of the problems before the next supervision session. These could include, for example, better adherence to employer and profession standards, a formal review of the size of your workload, increased frequency of supervision and additional development activities. These could perhaps include seeking a commitment to being supported on a specific development or training programme. It may be helpful to identify with your supervisor how supplementary supervision could be given from an external mentor or from a more experienced 'buddy' within your team or service.

If it has not been possible to successfully address the problems identified with your supervisor, it would be valuable to ask for a meeting with them and a valued colleague, trade union or professional association representative. An alternative is to ask to be joined by the supervisor's line manager. The problems may be ones that only a more senior manager can resolve, such as workload or professional development resources for both you and your supervisor. None of these are unusual requests, none are a last resort which should be feared, or a risk of being marked as a troublemaker.

Such meetings are far more frequent than is commonly assumed. What you are doing is acting as an appropriately assertive and confident professional who is determined to receive the effective support to enable you to practise safely and effectively.

If all else fails, you may decide to initiate the grievance procedures of the employer or blow the whistle to a senior person. It is not necessary to have the support of a trade union or professional association representative, the counsel and advice of a friend or colleague will be invaluable in maintaining your morale and direction.

None of these things may work. Sometimes people decide to leave the profession or take a break, but before doing this, ensure you have sought a resolution. You may decide to move to another team, specialism or employer. In doing this, it is important to be clear on the reasons and not move in desperation. A fresh start can be invigorating but it is important to be going to a good team with a good supervisor, in the kind of work and specialism which will excite and engage you.

The Supervisor

The first tough challenge for you to address as the supervisor is whether you are meeting the national professional standards and your employer's standards for supervision. If not, you need to be self-critical, checking your own practice. It is then important to identify and address the reasons why you are not matching these standards. If the issues relate to your own training as a supervisor (remember this is not the same as management training) or your own or the team's workload, only your line manager will be able to address this. You need to identify if you are allocating an appropriate quantity of work or complexity of work for the experience and capability of the social worker. The social worker's individual development plan needs to match their needs, the demands of the service and their professional aspirations.

It will be necessary for you to review and reflect on your concerns with your own line manager or professional mentor as part of your own professional supervision. This will give you the opportunity to plan resolutions, a record of what the organization may need to address and a route to organizational and cultural change. An intransigent culture of busy-itis, and lack of critical reflection can be even more endemic in senior management than the most hectic pressured team providing direct services!

One of the skills and attributes of a good supervisor is to create and maintain the 'sacred space' for reflective supervision, for professional learning. This applies to managing your own manager too. The space required is first of all in terms of time, for both preparing for, giving and following up work. The other space is the quietness and privacy of the room, with minimal interruptions.

The long-standing culture of general management, in which we are all working, plays down the professional expertise and knowledge of leaders. It may be that you personally, your organization or your employer, have invested in general management training which has led to your social work skills and knowledge (including practice research knowledge) becoming neglected. In particular, it is vital to receive good quality training as a supervisor of social workers and to have this regularly refreshed as part of continuing professional development and maintenance of registration.

At a personal level you may find it helpful to review how well you respect the professionalism and capability of the social worker. It is important to remember that they are a member of your own profession, they are a colleague. They have things to teach you and to help your own development. Wonnacott's methodology (2012: 148), described in Chapter 3, gives a good structure to start addressing problems without rushing in to blame, focusing from the outset on what can be done to achieve a positive outcome.

In the past, there has been a tendency to expect social workers at the start of their career to 'hit the ground running'. While it is important to have high expectations of social work education, we do not expect a newly qualified civil engineer to build a bridge without professional support or a new doctor to be able to undertake open heart surgery.

If you as the supervisor can be satisfied that you have provided good supervision, including access to tailored professional development, and you continue to have concerns about the quality of the work or conduct of the social worker, formal procedures will need to be mobilized. The investigations related to this will rigorously examine the professional supervision given. Great care needs to be taken to ensure that good quality supervision, professional support and development opportunities continue. There can be a risk that the Leviathan of personnel processes takes over and the individual's needs and those of the people receiving their services are overshadowed and neglected.

Notwithstanding the potential use of the disciplinary route, both you and the social worker, if the concerns have not been resolved, need to consider arranging a joint meeting with a third party to address the concerns, with the explicit aim of resolving the difficulties. You should separately and together consider whether the social worker is in the most appropriate position, and if not, what should be planned to achieve a move to a more appropriate role and work setting.

Problems and Solutions

Some of these may seem cheeky, but we as social workers need to be assertive, to take control and do our very best to get what we need from supervision in order for us to be able to give a good service.

Sometimes you have to do these things with a degree of humour, showing at the same time steely determination. Table 5.1 shows the problems and some possible solutions, if the supervision session is not turning out as you planned and hoped it would. This is not an exhaustive list, but gives a flavour of what are reasonable responses from you as a professional social worker.

Table 5.1 Problems and solutions

The problem	Solutions
Supervision always starts late or is cancelled at the last minute	Go to the session on time anyway, sit by your supervisor's desk, taking along paperwork or reading to keep you busy
	Leave a copy of your agenda for the supervision at the time the session was due to end
	Book a new session, do not wait until the next due date
	Offer unusual times of day which may be harder for them to avoid and which show your enthusiasm
The session is interrupted by telephone calls of knocks on the door	Make it plain this is not acceptable to you, for all but the most serious emergency such as serious illness or a 'blue light' crisis

Your supervisor focuses on the computer screen, electronic records and performance data, with no eye contact	Take control of the session from the outset
	Bring two copies of your written agenda for the session and be clear how much time and attention each item needs
	Be ready to physically turn the screen away from both of you or turn it off
Your supervisor never gets to the shared critical analysis and reflection part of the agenda	Insist on it, if necessary sit there until you are able to address it
	Be ready to show them how to do it
Your supervisor seems uninterested in your work or concerns	Inspire them, excite them with your enthusiasm, share with them what you have learned or the research you have read
	Give them some time and space to talk about their preoccupations and worries
You are dissatisfied with the opportunities you have for professional development	Ensure your requests are recorded and that you development plan includes them, even if the resources are not available
	Be ready to make your own arrangements for development and offer to share the cost and time with your employer
There is no supervision agreement and no records kept, despite you reminding the supervisor of this	Write your own agreement and make your own records and give your supervisor a copy

Good Practice Checklist: Options

✓ Maximize your use of supplementary supervision, see Chapter 3.
✓ Identify a particular social work colleague to use as a special buddy or mentor.
✓ Maintain a good network of social work colleagues and seek out professional development opportunities.
✓ Read professional journals, the latest books from the library and research sites (see Chapter 7).
✓ Discuss with colleagues what you are reading and in your team meetings.
✓ Keep copies of your agenda and your own notes from the supervision you receive and give your supervisor a copy.
✓ Keep challenging your lack of supervision, with your supervisor, their manager and with your professional organization.
✓ Do not convince yourself it is alright not to have supervision.

Problems in both the quality and delivery of supervision can be overcome, by both parties in supervision. It is important that neither of you avoids challenging the other, in terms of upholding your own professional standards, ensuring a good and safe service is provided and your rights to access continuing professional development. There are ways of supplementing unsatisfactory supervision, but this must not be at the cost of continuing to press for what is right or as an excuse for avoiding appropriate professional challenge from your designated supervisor. Even if you think you can manage without good reflective supervision (which you cannot!), it is wrong to expose less experienced colleagues who share your supervisor, to a continuing lack of access to this vital constituent part of social work.

6 Supervision in multi-disciplinary environments and supervision of non-professional staff

An increasing proportion of us are located in teams with other professions and where a proportion of the team may not have formal professional training. This is a positive change in that people using the service have direct access to a range of different skills and an integrated service. The challenge comes when our line manager may not be a social worker. Arrangements need to be made to ensure we have access to regular reflective supervision from a social worker and progressive continuing professional development as a social worker. It is also vital to build up and maintain a network of fellow social workers, to sustain our professional identity, to share learning and for mutual support.

Most of us are working alongside non-professional staff who are helping to provide the total 'package' of service for which we are responsible. It would be rare for you to be their line manager, nevertheless you have a lead position, either explicit or implicit, as the lead professional. Rather than wait for formal meetings like reviews, it is important to work together, with shared objectives and clarity on your respective responsibilities. In these situations you have a partly supervisory role which you need to acknowledge and own. On p. 93, the principles of delegation are examined in our work with these valuable colleagues.

SOCIAL WORK SUPERVISION WHERE THE LINE MANAGER IS NOT A SOCIAL WORKER

Formal 'off-line' supplementary supervision will be required, complemented by giving particular attention to building and maintaining a good peer network of social work colleagues for mentoring, consultation and keeping abreast of practice developments and knowledge.

For a growing number of social workers in integrated services, for example, in mental health and early intervention services for children and families, the line manager may not be a registered social worker. Statham (2003: 163) identifies for these managers the 'skilled task of ensuring access to professional supervision where this lies outside their own area of expertise and undertaking management of individuals and the team'. In these circumstances the triad of social worker, non-social worker line manager and professional social work supervisor needs to have a clear and recorded system for identifying respective accountabilities and review arrangements. The different and shared responsibilities of management and supervision explored in Chapter 2 can form the starting point for allocating who does what.

For those social workers working in integrated health and social care services, the National Health Service has a well-developed and growing culture of clinical governance. It arguably has a greater respect for the autonomy of health professionals, based on a greater consensus on their practice evidence base for effective and safe delivery of direct services. Clinical supervision is regarded as an integral component of clinical governance. It is defined as formal professional support and learning. The function is to enable health practitioners to progressively develop their knowledge and skills, to assume responsibility for their own practice and to enhance the care and safety of patients in complex clinical situations. With leadership and confident professional supervision, there is every opportunity for social work to join this culture of earning progressive autonomy. This entails taking responsibility for our own learning, while at the same time demonstrating our accountability for competent professional and effective practice through our continuing development of professional research-based knowledge and skill development.

Good Practice Checklist: Multi-Disciplinary Settings

✓ Insist on receiving 'off-line' supervision from a registered social worker if the line manager is not a registered social worker.

✓ If the employer is reluctant to facilitate this, explain the risks to maintaining continuing registration and the loss of the opportunity to continue to develop as a professional social worker.

✓ Retain professional registration and linked continuing and progressive professional development.

✓ Develop and sustain a peer group of fellow social work professionals at both a formal and informal level, to provide critical friends, informal mentoring and for moral and professional support.

✓ Regularly plan and review progressive professional development as a social worker with your line manager.

✓ While it would be good if the employer would fund or part-fund this, be ready to contribute at least some of the costs to retain professional status and to help ensure good preparation for your next career move in other social worker roles.

✓ Consider being active in, and directly contributing to, professional organizations.

✓ Spot how colleagues from other professions retain their professional identity and progressive professional development and follow their example.

The particular responsibilities which social workers often have for safeguarding children and vulnerable adults in these multi-disciplinary and multi-agency services require them to have ready and planned access to their professional supervisor in order that they have the reflective and analytical opportunity to make the complex judgements required and to make the necessary shared decisions.

Social workers in other kinds of multi-disciplinary teams, for example, schools, drug and alcohol misuse services, residential or day care services for adults or children will find a different and varying kind of commitment to professional development, reflective and analytical supervision and progression within particular professions. The skills and particular attributes of the social worker members within the multi-disciplinary team are likely to be greatly valued but there may be little recognition of the particular and specific professional and development needs.

In the cases where employers have few social work staff and line managers are not social workers, how can the employer and line manager support the social worker to find the satisfaction of supervision and professional development?

■ Having decided to recruit a registered social worker, it is important to recognize them as such and support their professional development and continuing registration.

■ Make arrangements for them to receive regular formal supervision from a registered social worker.

■ Ensure that their line manager and their social work supervisor have clarity on their respective and shared responsibilities and that there are regular, recorded three-way face-to-face review meetings with the social worker.

■ Be ready to support participation in social work-specific continuing professional development, including the Assessed and Supported Year of Employment and modules of the post-qualifying awards, in terms of time and fees. Note these costs may need to be shared with the social worker.

- Provide the time and training resources required for them to retain their professional registration.
- Identify areas of work in which the social worker needs to have experience to develop and retain their social work skills and to demonstrate progression in the Professional Development Framework (Social Work Reform Board 2010), and facilitate access to this work experience with other local employers of social worker.
- If the organization decides not to recognize them as registered social workers within their responsibilities and role as an employee, it is necessary to determine the willingness and ability to support their professional development, continuing registration and active maintenance of a professional peer network. It is important for them not to lose their professional registration and the benefits to the service will be substantial in terms of their growing knowledge and skill and any future service development.
- Facilitate and support them to develop and maintain a professional social work peer network.
- Adapt the organization's procedures on continuing professional development to facilitate their progression within the social work profession, both in the Professional Capabilities Framework and modular post-qualifying awards.
- Arrange that all social workers should receive supervision to the standards, see Chapter 3, from a registered social worker who is experienced and knowledgeable in their particular area of work.

ALLOCATING RESPONSIBILITIES IN WORKING WITH SUPPORT AND NON-PROFESSIONAL STAFF

Most social workers are located in services and teams which include support or non-professional social care staff. These colleagues may share the same manager, or work in another service within the organization, and there is shared responsibility for work with individual vulnerable adults, children and families. In these situations, the social worker will almost certainly have responsibility for the care plan and the lead professional accountability, although they may not directly supervise these staff in a managerial sense. Nevertheless, as the accountable registered professional, they have the responsibility to oversee the work, to ensure they are working in harmony and to a common purpose. This is a substantial, but unavoidable responsibility which comes early, and often unrecognized, in the professional life of a social worker, when they are learning to take responsibility for their own practice and are gaining confidence in their own skills. While there may be a difference in life experience and in experience in the service area, the social worker has greater responsibilities and personal accountability.

It is too much to assume co-working, informal discussions or waiting for case reviews will ensure a cohesive and competent service will be provided. The shared plan for providing a service, which may include continuing assessment, managing risks, seeking changes in behaviour, increasing independence and substantial emotional and practical support, needs to be focused, skilful and provided in a seamless way.

In order for this to be successful, clarity is required on the arrangements for the following:

- delegation
- supervision
- professional support
- case accountability
- care planning and review
- recording and sharing of records
- providing specific training or development opportunities for the support worker
- addressing disagreements.

PRINCIPLES OF DELEGATION TO NON-PROFESSIONAL STAFF FOR SOCIAL WORKERS

A group of colleges of health professions have undertaken some very helpful work on the supervision, accountability and delegation of activities to support workers (Chartered Society of Physiotherapy et al. 2006). Building on this work, the following structured model is helpful in clarifying roles and accountabilities, to avoid confusion about who is responsible for what and to ensure an effective service is delivered.

- The registered social worker undertakes the assessment, planning, implementation and evaluation of the delegated role.
- The person to whom the tasks are delegated must have an appropriate role, level of experience and competence to carry them out.
- Registered social workers must not delegate tasks and responsibilities to colleagues that are beyond their level of skill and experience.
- The support worker should undertake training to ensure competence in carrying out any tasks required. Their line manager and employer are responsible for ensuring this is provided.
- The tasks to be delegated must be discussed by the social worker with the support worker to ensure both are confident that the work can be carried out.
- The level of supervision and feedback provided is appropriate to the work being delegated.
- Recording is regularly considered and reviewed.
- Regular supervision is planned and adhered to.
- There is open access for the support worker to informal advice and support from the social worker.
- The support worker will be expected to make decisions within the care plan agreed and seek advice where needed.

This may seem quite formal but it is important to avoid confusion or a disorganized service. Any care plan or intervention plan needs to be well organized and coherent for the people we serve, their families and carers. In integrated services and multi-disciplinary settings, supervision arrangements for non-professional staff may vary; these must be clear and rigorous in order to ensure that the work is carried out in as seamless a way as possible with explicit accountabilities and responsibilities.

WORKING AS COLLEAGUES

The wide range of support workers and non-professional staff who provide the level and range of help needed in children's services and adult social care are colleagues and are vital to the overall effectiveness of the services being given. Some of these colleagues are based within discrete services like residential care, home care, supported housing and children's centres. In these situations the work to be undertaken as part of the social worker's care plan needs to be agreed at a formal level between the social worker and the manager of that service. It would be wrong to assume that the work would be undertaken simply on the basis of a discussion. Case conferences and formal reviews can provide the structure and record required to ensure effective work is undertaken and allocation of responsibilities is clear. However, it is the day-by-day and week-by-week working together which is critical and needs to be unified and effectively led and overseen.

Social workers early in their career, or not experienced in the specialist area where the support worker is based, may be reticent about specifying, leading, planning and reviewing the shared work. However, professionally, they have accountabilities for the work and quickly grow in confidence as professionals with substantial responsibilities. They need to respect their support worker colleagues, listen to their feedback and experience in the context of their overall responsibilities. Equally, the line managers of the support workers must 'allow' work to be appropriately delegated and supervised. Loose terms like 'provide support' and 'supervise' in care plans for delegated work need to be avoided to ensure that there is purposeful and active work and help being provided.

The social worker needs to be clear on the respective responsibilities of their own line manager and the manager of the other staff, if different. There needs to be an explicit plan of the work to be undertaken by each worker, acknowledging and respecting the particular skills and experience of the non-professional worker. In addition, they may have wider responsibilities, for example, the needs of other people living in group settings, like supported housing or residential care. In these circumstances these responsibilities have to be not only acknowledged but also respected.

CONCLUSION

Social workers, as they become more experienced, confident and authoritative, will find themselves called upon by less experienced and non-social worker colleagues to provide advice, support and informal supervision. This is to be welcomed and acknowledged by employers, managers and supervisors. This is an area of work which social workers and their supervisors need to address and review in supervision.

To work in a multi-disciplinary environment can be both stimulating and professionally isolating. Regular professional reflective supervision from a social worker is crucial and imperative. Equally, access to progressive continuing professional development as a social worker must be maintained, alongside a group of social work peers. In working alongside non-professional colleagues, where you share the work with an individual or family, your own leadership and quasi-supervisory responsibilities need to be explored and recorded in order that together you can provide a cohesive and effective service.

Working in these ways extends our responsibilities, requiring a secure sense of our own specific skills and working methods we bring to working as part of a team of different kinds of colleagues. It requires a heightened clarity of how we work to achieve change and how we are accountable. These are the reasons why regular and structured professional reflective supervision is even more vital in these settings.

7 Further reading and resources

Once qualified, one of the losses is easy access to a library for both old and new texts, specialist journals and research. Maintaining the momentum of keeping abreast of research and policy changes is important. There is much general social care and children's services material available, it can be a little harder to access specific social work literature and research. Offices where social workers are based vary enormously in the visibility of books, the use of knowledge websites and research material. It is valuable to bring copies of material you have found useful to form a small team library or reading basket. You can volunteer to present some research of new practice ideas at a team meeting. Some employers used the national funding for the newly qualified social workers pilot programme to buy a small bundle of books for all of them on appointment. A relatively low cost welcome and greatly valued, setting the course for a career-long habit of reading and continuing learning.

LIBRARIES

- Many organizations have their own libraries for staff and some social work teams purchase and share books.
- Most of the newer universities have free reading access to their libraries and electronic access to journals.
- Public libraries will order any book to borrow for a modest fee.

USING THE WEB

Keeping abreast of current research, commentaries on practice and policy changes can be made easy by regularly scanning key websites or joining their 'emailing lists':

- British Association of Social Workers services for members.
- Care Knowledge, your employer is likely to be a subscriber if the OLM Care First electronic case records system is used.
- College of Social Work e-library for members of the College.
- Community Care Inform, subscriber service.
- Research in Practice and Research in Practice for Adults, check if your employing organisation is a member.
- Social Care Institute for Excellence (SCIE) offers free internet access to a range of social care research and publications.

PROFESSIONAL STANDARDS

The Codes of Practice for social workers and employers of social workers in the four UK nations are important reference documents:

- General Social Care Council England (2010) *Codes of Practice for Social Care Workers and Employers of Social Care Workers*. London: General Social Care Council, to be held by Skills for Care following the closure of the Council.
- Care Council for Wales (2003) *Codes of Practice for Social Care Workers and Employers of Social Care Workers*. Cardiff: Care Council for Wales.
- Northern Ireland Social Care Council (2002) *Codes of Practice for Social Care Workers and Social Care Employers*. Belfast: Northern Ireland Social Care Council.
- Scottish Social Services Council (2004) *Codes of Practice for Social Services Workers and Employers of Social Services Workers*. Dundee: Scottish Social Services Council.

The British Association of Social Workers policies are all available to view and download from the website:

- Supervision Policy 2011
- Continuing Professional Development Policy 2012
- Code of Ethics 2012.

JOURNALS AND MAGAZINES

The British Association for Adoption and Fostering publishes *Adoption and Fostering*, a quarterly journal free to member organizations and by subscription. If your organization is involved in this work, a copy should be available.

The British Association of Social Workers publications are:

- *Professional Social Work*, free to members
- *Practice Journal*, subscription or library access
- *British Journal of Social Work*, subscription or library access

Care Knowledge, if your employer is a subscriber, this gives access to a range of relevant professional journals.

Another useful source of information is *Community Care*, an e-magazine, freely available online, along with a wide range of information and online discussion opportunities.

Other useful resources include:

- 'Inform' is an electronic library of special reports and practice guides by subscription.
- *Research in Practice*, www.rip.org.uk, which offers free access to member organizations, and supports-evidence informed practice with children and families.
- *Research in Practice for Adults*, www.ripfa.org.uk, which offers free access to member organizations, and supports evidence-informed practice with adult social care and health.

■ The College of Social Work is an e-magazine, free to members, and offers access to ebooks and journals.

FURTHER READING

Donnellan, H. and Jack, G. (2010) *The Survivors Guide for Newly Qualified Child and Families Social Workers*. London: Jessica Kingsley.

Galpin, D., Bigmore, J. and Parker, J. (2012) *The Survival Guide for Newly Qualified Social Workers in Adult and Mental Health Services*. London: Jessica Kingsley.

Gould, N. and Baldwin, M. (eds) (2004) *Social Work, Critical Reflection and the Learning Organisation*. Aldershot: Ashgate.

Morrison, T. (2005) *Strength to Strength: A Facilitator's Guide to Preparing Supervisees, Students and Trainees for Supervision*. Brighton: Pavilion.

Newman, A., Moseley, A., Tierney, S. and Ellis, A. (2005) *Evidence-Based Social Work: A Guide for the Perplexed*. Lyme Regis: Russell House Publishing.

Orme, J. and Shemmings, D. (2011) *Developing Research Based Social Work Practice*. Basingstoke: Palgrave Macmillan.

Rutter, L. and Brown, K. (2012) *Critical Thinking and Professional Judgement for Social Work*. London: Sage.

Thompson, N. (2006) *Promoting Workplace Learning*. Bristol: The Policy Press.

Wonnacott, J. (2012) *Mastering Social Work Supervision*. London: Jessica Kingsley.

Glossary

Case management: This is a three-stage process. First, the assessment of the needs and circumstances of a person, including those of their carers, followed by negotiating and arranging services, in agreement with them, to meet these needs, subject to available resources (or matching the eligibility criteria or priorities of the services). The third stage is the implementation of the provision of these services, monitoring and reviewing the outcomes and quality and any revision which may be necessary. The origin of this way of describing how social services are provided comes from the community care reforms at the end of the 1980s. When applied to social work, it is silent on the active, direct work of the social worker, beyond assessing, arranging services and review. Arguably, it simply describes a generic process which could apply to car repairs or computer maintenance services.

The knowledge the social worker uses is found in the effects of ageing, disability, mental health, what works in promoting independence and rehabilitation. The skills used are in advocacy, promoting rights, counselling, mediation, working with family groups and helping people and their carers navigate the available services.

Continuing professional development: This is the planned and progressive development of practice skills and knowledge which takes place throughout a social worker's career. It includes the full range of learning activities, including professional supervision, peer group learning, personal study, training programmes and higher level qualifications. It is both an entitlement as an employed professional *and* a personal responsibility, requiring the commitment and resources of the individual social worker. It should be more ambitious than simply retaining professional registration, the aim is to extend and develop our skills and knowledge throughout our working lives. The knowledge acquired includes current research which informs evidence-based practice. The training, education and learning which form part of continuing professional development should be validated if at all possible, in order that it can demonstrate and provide evidence for career progression and for modular post-qualifying awards, jointly awarded in partnership with universities.

Critical analysis: This is the thoughtful and logical analysis of the information available to the social worker and their supervisor, including identifying feelings and emotions. It includes asking questions, building and rehearsing arguments, exploring and developing solutions to problems, evaluating potential lessons from research and experience and articulating clearly what the problem is and the planned solutions.

Because social workers work with complexity, uncertainty and risk, straightforward answers and solutions are rarely available. Careful and shared analysis, which takes time and energy, is a vital component of the way we need to work and learn.

Earned autonomy: Autonomy means independence, freedom or self-determination. It can also mean 'self-governing'. Most social workers would not describe their practice in their working environment as autonomous, with much of the procedures prescribed in national or local regulation. Equally, most of us would question whether we should be free to independently and unaccountably determine all of our judgements and actions. However, as we can demonstrate our growing evidence base of effective practice and full ownership of our professional development, a greater degree of autonomy can be earned as we are trusted to be competent. Some of this will require changes in the regulation of statutory services, as suggested by the Munro Review. While we may feel our professional autonomy is curtailed, perhaps by legal process, decisions being taken at panels and meetings or by limited resources, the individual and families we work with often see us as very powerful individuals with a great degree of personal discretion and authority to act alone.

Social work has not sought to be 'self-governing'. In pressing for professional registration and regulation, we were clear this should be undertaken by a body not dominated by social workers. There are potentially some functions which the College of Social Work could undertake, with responsibilities delegated by government. It could take authority unto itself. However, at the current stage of its development it is undertaking work and making decisions without a membership; it is too early to judge if it will have the capacity for self-governance by the profession or a mandate from members of the profession.

Earned autonomy comes from demonstrating our ability to make sound decisions in practising as social workers, based on a high level of skill and knowledge founded on reliable research evidence and taking personal responsibility for our own professional development in reflective supervision, where we are able and willing to demonstrate our capability and to be accountable for the best standards of practice for the people we serve and their carers.

Graduateness and master's level: Social work education and the professional qualification are achieved at both honours degree (graduate) and master's level. Most post-qualifying awards are achieved at master's level. It is useful to understand the characteristics of these in order to remember and respect how we have arrived at our professional roles, what can continue to be expected of us and what our supervisor and leaders should expect and respect in us in our work.

The characteristics of graduateness are identified as knowledge focused in a discipline of study, reflexivity, the capacity to reflect on actions in order to engage in a process of continuous learning, managing tasks, solving problems, working with others, communication skills, self-awareness and the ability to self-evaluate. The characteristics of master's level in addition to these include systematic understanding of knowledge at the forefront of the discipline, demonstrating originality in the application of knowledge and in how we address problems.

In the commotion of our busy working life, with limited access to professional learning and current research information, surrounded by processes which constrain how we work and a management culture, which may undervalue our professional skills and focus on performance targets, it can be difficult to hold on to our level of competence attained at qualification. The style and content of our supervision should be built on moving beyond this base standard of competence. We need to enter the supervision session with clear expectations of ourselves at these levels and above.

Learning organization: We should expect all organizations to use all of the skills and initiative of their staff and to learn from them how their services may be made better. A 'learning organization' will take positive steps to invest in all its workforce and to listen carefully to ideas about how the services it provides can be improved. A learning organization will invest in the development of staff skills and knowledge, it will ensure they have the opportunity to reflect on how they are working and will wish to be open to learning from everyone who works in the organization. This requires open systems of communication across all levels of management, in quality assurance systems, and ensures innovation is welcomed and developed.

Supervision provides a conduit or process for communicating new and different ideas and developments in social work service and the facility for rigorous evaluation of what works, and what does not.

Managerialism: This is the belief that there are common ways of organizing and delivering any service, focusing on direction, efficiency, external accountability and externally defined standards. It is centred on developing the skills and focus of senior staff on this agenda, rather than the professional skills to lead and provide the service.

For social work, alongside many other services provided for the public, it has been an experience which has ignored or under-valued the expertise and professional judgement of social workers. The focus on managing performance indicators, by which services are measured and inspected, has emphasized nationally prescribed processes, rather than trusting professional judgement and discretion.

The response by the competent social work professional needs to be openness to scrutiny, the sharing of our evidence base for practice and demonstrating good outcomes for the people we serve and for their carers. The managerialist agenda of performance indicators and finite budgets have value, they are part of the core concerns of managers, it is important to recognize and respect this. However, indicators only indicate and tough decisions about resources are part of everyday prioritizations, just as all social workers have to make decisions about how to use their time. The professional social worker is entering supervision to develop and sustain their practice, to achieve the best results for their work. The managerial agenda is part of the context which requires mediation and brokering. When it dominates, then our practice is diminished and our work is devalued. The skilled supervisor mediates these tensions, keeping professional skills and judgements to the fore.

The Munro Review: Professor Eileen Munro was commissioned by the Secretary of State for Education, Michael Gove, in 2010 to undertake an independent review of child protection in England. Her third and final report, *A Child-centred System*, published in 2011, should have a radical effect on how social workers are prepared for and supported in working with greater discretion and respect for their professional judgements. Her review found that over-bureaucratization and focus on prescribed process have limited the potential effectiveness of social work interventions. The review makes the case for radically improving the knowledge and skills of social workers from initial training, through continuing professional development. This includes making better use of research evidence for effective practice.

Post-qualifying Awards: These are provided by universities working in partnership with social work employers, currently at three levels: specialist, higher specialist and advanced levels. These are available in modular form and can be undertaken in a variety of flexible ways, either with the support of your employer or by independent study. It is likely these awards will become even more important and widely used as the aspirations and expectations of social workers are raised and there is a greater need to assure the skills and capabilities of senior social work professionals.

Reflection: There are two meanings which are important in supervision. The first is the examination of our practice to uncover assumptions which are hidden or unspoken. It enables us to analyse our intuitive judgements or 'hunches' which are invaluable. If we are clear in our analysis and can be articulate in supervision, we can share our reflections on the information available and the ways in which we are working with risk and the different methods of social work intervention we are using. We can explore and evaluate our practice against relevant research and change and develop how we work.

Related terms are reflexivity and reflexiveness and these are used to describe how we process information and make choices and decisions, an examination of cause and effect. For supervision, it can be a way of describing how we internalize and systematize good habits of critical analysis and reflective practice, not only in supervision but also while we are out doing the busy business of social work.

The second meaning comes from the psychotherapeutic tradition of social work where emotions and feelings are transferred (see **transference**) or reflected onto another person or situation.

Social Work Reform Board: The Board was appointed by the government to implement the recommendations of the Social Work Taskforce, which itself was set up by the government following the serious concerns of the public and within the profession following child protection tragedies. The focus is on improving front line social work practice and management. It has been working on delivering a range of work, including employer standards, workforce planning, career development and a professional capabilities framework for social work. Current information on how this work is progressing is available on the Social Work Reform Board and the College of Social Work websites.

Therapeutic imperative: Social work is about achieving change, despite the focus in some social work settings on making assessments to decide whether a service, provided by someone else, should be given or not. Even in these circumstances, as the social worker, we are responsible for forming a relationship with the person and their carers, demonstrating an understanding of where they are and working with them to identify how their needs can be met and their wishes and feelings are respected and used. Social work has a long tradition of therapeutic interventions based on forming positive relationships which can be used to increase insight, to address historical grief, to test and use different ways of relating to others and addressing emotions. This runs alongside the other two social work traditions of *transforming* how services are provided, how people who may be excluded are treated, the tradition of social action and the *social order* function of reducing troublesome behaviour, restoring social stability and managing risk.

Doing social work is purposeful and focused, with clear objectives and interventions based on the social worker's own skills in relationship-based therapeutic interventions. This cannot be delegated to others, even if they have specific contributions to an overall plan of care. If we as social workers do not think we can have a direct impact and make a positive contribution, we are not working as social workers. This is not to under-estimate the value of the advice, guidance, consultation and co-working we can offer professional colleagues and carers where we may not take on full case responsibility.

Part of the function of supervision is to identify, articulate and evaluate the positive, therapeutic and change-focused work that we can and do undertake as social workers.

Transference: This is the initially unconscious, redirection or reflection of feelings and emotions from one person to another. It comes from the psychotherapeutic and psychodynamic roots of social work. It is an important component of professional, reflective social work supervision. While transference is unconscious, it may be seen as irrational, but when uncovered and understood, it can be a way of giving meaning or understanding to powerful and often painful experiences. These dynamics and placing of feelings and emotions may be awakened or re-enacted in the relationship of the supervisor and supervisee. Where they come from the work, it gives a potent source of material to be examined, analysed and used. Where it comes from relationships outside work, it is probably best addressed more privately with colleagues, friends and other personal support networks. Transference will be observed and experienced in our work with the people we serve and their families and can form useful areas of direct work with them to help them understand, gain insight and move on to make choices about change.

The emotions experienced and generated in our work are important sources of information for our practice. They are also emotions which have to be understood, addressed by us, and used as a source of learning.

References

Adams, R. (2002) *Social Policy for Social Work*. Basingstoke: Palgrave.

Baginsky, M., Moriarty, J., Manthorpe, J. et al. (2009) *Social Workers Workload Survey: Messages from the Frontline*. London: Social Work Taskforce.

Beresford, P., Flemming, J., Glynn, H. et al. (2011) *Supporting People: Towards a Person-Centred Approach*. Bristol: The Policy Press.

Bishop, V. (ed.) (2007) *Clinical Supervision in Practice*. Basingstoke: Palgrave Macmillan.

Bond, T. et al. (2010) *Ethical Framework for Good Practice in Counselling and Psychotherapy*. Lutterworth: British Association for Counselling and Psychotherapy.

British Association of Social Workers (2011) *Code of Ethics*. Birmingham: British Association of Social Workers.

Brown, K. (2011) *Evaluation Report for Hampshire County Council: Introduction to Leadership and Management: Improving Personal and Organisational Performance Programme*. Bournemouth: Bournemouth University.

Burnham, D. (2011) Selective memory: a note on social work historiography, *British Journal of Social Work*, 41(1): 5–21.

Carpenter, J., McLaughlin, H., Patsios, D. et al. (2010) *Newly Qualified Social Worker Programme: Evaluation Report on the First Year, 2008–09*. Leeds: Children's Workforce Development Council.

Chard, A. and Ayre, P. (2010) Managerialism: at the tipping point, in P. Ayre and M. Preston-Shoot (eds) *Children's Services at the Crossroads: A Critical Evaluation of Contemporary Policy for Practice*. Lyme Regis: Russell House Publishing.

Chartered Society of Physiotherapy, Royal College of Speech and Language Therapists, British Dietetic Association, and Royal College of Nursing (2006) *Supervision, Accountability and Delegation of Activities: A Guide for Registered Practitioners and Support Workers*. London: Chartered Society of Physiotherapy, Royal College of Speech and Language Therapists, British Dietetic Association, Royal College of Nursing.

Cope, D. (2010) *Supervising Career Grade Psychiatrists in Managed Settings*. London: Royal College of Psychiatrists.

Davies, P. and Bynner, J. (1999) *The Impact of Credit Based Systems on Learning Cultures*. ESRC, Report of the Learning Society Programme, available at: www.regard.ac.uk.

Department for Education and Skills (2006) *Championing Children: A Shared Set of Skills, Knowledge and Behaviours for Those Leading and Managing Integrated Children's Services*. London: Department for Education and Skills.

Donnellan, H. and Jack, G. (2010) *The Survival Guide for Newly Qualified Child and Family Social Workers: Hitting the Ground Running*. London: Jessica Kingsley Publishers.

Evans, T. (2009) Managing to be professional? Team managers and practitioners in social services, in J. Harris and V. White (eds) *Modernising Social Work*. Bristol: The Policy Press.

Farmer, E.R.G. (2009) Reunification with birth families, in G. Schofield and J. Simmonds (eds) *The Child Placement Handbook*. London: British Association for Adoption and Fostering.

General Social Care Council (2010) *Specialist Standards and Requirements for Post Qualifying Social Work Education and Training, Leadership and Management*. London: General Social Care Council.

Gordon, R. and Hendry, E. (2001) Supervising assessments of children and families: the role of the front line manager, in J. Howarth (ed.) *The Child's World: Assessing Children in Need*. London: Jessica Kingsley Publishers.

Gould, N. and Baldwin, M. (2004) *Social Work, Critical Reflection and the Learning Organisation*. Aldershot: Ashgate.

Jones, M. (2004) Supervision, learning and transformative practices, in N. Gould and M. Baldwin, (eds) *Social Work, Critical Reflection and the Learning Organization*. Aldershot: Ashgate.

Kadushin, A. (1976) *Supervision in Social Work*. New York: Columbia University Press.

Luckock, B., Lefevre, M., Orr, D. and Jones, M. (2006) *Teaching, Learning and Assessing Communication Skills with Children and Young People in Social Work Education*. London: Social Care Institute for Excellence.

MacDonnell, F. (2011) *The College of Social Work Supervision Policy*. Birmingham: British Association of Social Workers, The College of Social Work.

Mattinson, J. (1975) *The Reflection Process in Casework Supervision*. London: Institute of Marital Studies, the Tavistock Institute of Human Relations.

McKitterick, W. (2009) *The Future for Social Workers in Adult Services: Professional Social Work*. Birmingham: British Association of Social Workers.

McKitterick, W. (2009–11) *Newly Qualified Social Worker Pilot Programme, Annual Employer Support Reports for the Children's Workforce Development Council*. Cambridge: Cambridge Education.

Morrison, T. (2005) *Strength to Strength: A Facilitator's Guide to Preparing Supervisees, Students and Trainees for Supervision*. Brighton: Pavilion.

Munro, E. (2011) *The Munro Review of Child Protection Final Report: A Child-Centred System*. London: Department for Education.

National College for Leadership of Schools and Children's Services (2011) *Qualities Framework for Directors and Senior Leaders of Children's Services*. London: National College for Leadership of Schools and Children's Services.

Newman, H. ([1852]1997) *The Idea of a University*. Washington, DC: Regnery.

Oakeshott, M. (1989) *The Voice of Liberal Learning*. New Haven, CT: Yale University Press.

Ofsted (2008) *Joint Area Review: Haringey Children's Services Authority Area*. London: Ofsted, Health Care Commission, HM Inspectorate of Constabulary.

Ofsted (2012) *High Expectations, High Support and High Challenge, Protecting Children More Effectively Through Better Support for Front Line Social Work Practice*. London: Ofsted.

Ross, G.M. (2011) *What's the Use of Lectures?: Forty years on. Discourse* 10(3), available at: http://www.philosophy.leeds.ac.uk/GMR/articles/What's%20the%20use%20of%20lectures-5.pdf.

Skills for Care (2009) *Occupational Standards for Leadership and Management of Care Services*. Leeds: Skills for Care.

Social Work Reform Board (2010) *Building a Safe and Confident Future: One Year On*. London: Social Work Reform Board.

Social Work Reform Board (2011) *Standards for Employers and Supervision Framework*. London: Social Work Reform Board.

Social Work Taskforce (2009) *Building a Safe and Confident Future*. London: Department for Education.

Statham, D. (ed.) (2003) *Managing Front Line Practice in Social Care*. London: Jessica Kingsley.

Stevenson, O. (2010) Foreword, in J. Carpenter et al. (eds) *Newly Qualified Social Worker Programme: Evaluation Report on the First Year, 2008–09*. Leeds: Children's Workforce Development Council.

Sharpe, E., Moriarty, J., Stevens, M., Manthorpe, J. and Hussein, S. (2011) *Into the Workforce: Report from a Study of New Social Work Graduates*. London: Social Care Workforce Research Unit, Kings College London.

Tsui, M. (2005) *Social Work Supervision: Contexts and Concepts*. London: Sage.

White, S. (2008) Discourse analysis and reflexivity, in M. Gray and S.A. Webb (eds) *Thinking about Social Work: Theories and Methods for Practice*. London: Sage.

Wonnacott, J. (2012) *Mastering Social Work Supervision*. London: Jessica Kingsley.

Index